DOG MYTHS:

What You Believe about DOGS can come back to BITE You!

for
Riley
&
Riley !

Socialize for Success!

Garrett Stevens

This book is dedicated to all the dogs and, specifically, to my own furry companions, Bosley and Rambo.
Thanks for teaching me the way of dogs.

Library of Congress Control Number: 2018900487

ISBN: 978-0-9997735-4-3

Printed in the United States of America

"Whenever you find yourself on the side of the majority, it is time to reform."

- Mark Twain

"The quality of your life is nothing but the quality of the questions you ask."

- Tony Robbins

"The electric light did not come from the continuous improvement of candles."

- Oren Harari

Dog:

-A domesticated carnivorous mammal that typically has a long snout, an acute sense of smell, and a barking, howling, or whining voice. It is <u>widely kept as a pet</u> or for work or field sports.

Myth:

-A <u>traditional story</u>, especially one concerning the history of a people or explaining some natural or social phenomenon, and typically involving supernatural beings or events.

-A <u>widely held but</u> <u>false</u> belief or idea.

TABLE OF CONTENTS

INTRODUCTION

"I therefore claim to show, not how men think in myths, but how myths operate in men's minds without their being aware of the fact." -Claude Levi Strauss

What we believe and the stories we tell ourselves and tell to others are quite powerful. Our thoughts are very real things. The questions we ask influence and direct our thinking and our actions for better or for worse. This in turn affects others. This affects our dogs. This affects our behavior and their behavior.

Believing behavioral myths about our dogs and their specific language and behavior, no matter how ubiquitous, divorces us from a healthy and genuine relationship with them! Belief in these widespread dog myths is what separates us from honest interspecies communication and what gives behavioral problems a foothold. If we give credence to any of these myths, however rampant they may run throughout societies across the globe, we mentally drive a great wedge of misunderstanding between our two species.

Masses of well-meaning dog owners and scores of professionals in the dog industry could benefit significantly if one were able to clearly define these generally accepted yet disastrous dog myths. As the saying goes, the truth will set you free.

We are in need of a large warning sign. Dog owners and professionals in the field need a straightforward "Do NOT Do" list just as we need a concise "To Do" list. In this way many an atrocious dog behavioral problem could be prevented at the outset with a new puppy and/or efficiently and readily altered in the older dog or rescue dog that displays unsocial or undesirable behavior.

If someone was able to go beyond what is the norm and look past the status quo dog training and behavioral modification methods of today then the potential exists to unwind our domesticated dog's language and training as it pertains to their daily interaction with us. That, Dear Reader, is what I am attempting here. I hope this book will be a veritable treasure map of previously uncovered dog communication that you can follow.

There are several rather wild and somewhat foolhardy beliefs the greater part of loving dog-owners cling to concerning their beloved dogs. These beliefs, these old wives' tales and this pervasive dog mythology, can be quite harmful if one remains in the dark. The largest part of dog owners and dog professionals, I've come to realize, are unaware of the various dog myths that plague our society! In this book I will attempt to shed some much needed light upon the gloom that is our own human behavior and interactions with our dogs and pups and upon the persistently common yet unbeneficial training methods we apply toward our pets. We must be curious enough, honest enough, and bold enough to ask the tough questions as we explore our dogs and pups, their behavior, and the elaborate social customs that our dogs use to manipulate control in our homes and in our relationships as they daily interact with us.

There has never been a time in human history where we have access to as much information as right now. Much of it amounts to so much noise. We have limitless information, demonstration, internet articles, YouTube videos, professional animal behaviorists, professional dog trainers, part-time dog trainers, lay people claiming to be trainers, veterinarian counsel, podcasts about dogs, magazines about dogs and pups, and TV shows that feature dog training, puppy conditioning, animal communication, dog psychics, dog whispering, dog daycare, dog boarding, dog rescue, dog sports, and several other forms of what I like to call "dog mania." But despite all that <u>did you know that dog aggression, dog fear and phobias, and behavioral issues are on the rise? Did you know dogs are biting more people nowadays than a few years ago</u>?

What the heck is going on? Why have bites been on the rise? Why is aggression and fear so prevalent? If we, as people, in this modern world that we've created, know so very much and have access to unlimited information about our dogs, why do I see terrified and aggressive dogs every day of my life? If one were to take a stroll around a suburban neighborhood or visit a busy walk spot or park downtown, evidence of problematic doggy drama would soon appear before you. The astute observer can bear witness to unhappy and unbalanced dogs and shoddy training methods throughout their entire day! What is happening in our society at large? What is happening with our dogs?

Dogs are rebelling. They rebel against how we treat them and how we train them. They are rebels with a cause. A good cause at that; their cause is to be understood. Understanding begins with our beliefs about dogs. It starts with us and with our thinking. It starts with our many wives' tales. It starts with what we think we know about our puppies and our dogs. It starts with our myths.

"The most useful piece of learning for the uses of life is to <u>un</u>learn what is <u>un</u>true." - Antisthenes

If you haven't been a former client of ours you probably did not know that <u>the entire premise of dog training and behavior modification literally **goes against** Mother Nature's calming ways and can often lead to more behavioral issues later in a dog's life</u>! Yes, it's true. Nearly all forms of dog training and behavior modification go directly against how the mother and father dog would <u>calmly</u> and naturally raise and equip their pups! Industry standards often go against how any older social canine would deal with a younger canine. Please think about that for a moment. The greater part of dog training and dog behavior modification as

taught by professionals throughout the industry, as it is now, across the board, can, and in my experience dealing with countless clients who've tried these mainstream methods, <u>often does lead to worse future behavior in scores of dogs</u>! That is essentially one of the central themes that my first two books examine because there is such a need for people to identify and hopefully awaken to this truth. There is such a need for better methods of behavior modification.

"Honesty is the first chapter in the book of wisdom." - Thomas Jefferson

In Dog Myths we investigate and honestly explain why the mainstream dog myths and false beliefs and narratives that plague our society need to be clearly rebutted in order to make way for superior connections and enhanced interactions with our dogs and their behavior. It starts with understanding. We need to rebuke these dog myths in order to see the truth and have a healthy and honest relationship with our dogs. We need to address these common myths concerning our dogs' body language. In the book I also try to equip the reader with straightforward, real world solutions based in dog movement and communication. These helpful tips are found at the end of each chapter.

If it were possible to define and address these numerous dog myths one could prevent or reverse behavior problems and streamline efficiency in the whole dog training industry. That is what I am attempting to do with this book. Please be aware: people consider these myths as truth. Masses of fine people permit these myths and falsities wholehearted access into their minds even if NO dog on the planet would ever fall for or believe them!

We act upon what we believe. These commonly accepted myths about our dogs can and quite often do come back to bite the believer (or a hapless neighbor, family member, or friend) in the butt!

Dear Reader,

I want to thank you at the outset for reading this book with an open mind and an intrepid spirit. I sincerely hope you enjoy it and that, together, we can build a brighter future with a greater understanding of our dogs, their amazing language, and their wonderful social and parenting skills. Beware: this book is dangerous! Confronting myths is no laughing matter. There be psychological dragons here!

-G

CHAPTER 1 – MYTH 1

-An excited dog is a happy dog

-My dog is happy when he's excited

"Science must begin with myths and with the criticism of myths." – Karl Popper

Webster's defines **happiness** as good fortune, prosperity; a state of well-being and contentment: joy. It is a pleasurable or satisfying experience. Felicity.

My friend, Shawn Achor, one of the world's leading experts on the link between our happiness and success, and New York Times best-selling author of *The Happiness Advantage* and *Before Happiness*, obviously has much expertise in the happiness arena. His TED talk has over 13 million views. Shawn is the leading positive psychology strategist. He says, "So many people are struggling to find happiness while their brain is inundated by noise. If your brain is receiving too much information, it automatically thinks you're under threat and scans the world for the negative first. Because the brain is limited, whatever you attend to first becomes your reality."

I agree with him. Our brains are indeed inundated with noise. Our brains are loaded with puppy propaganda! There is so much bad information about puppies and dogs online, in books, and in our minds. There is a daily deluge of dog mythology spewing out of both professional and lay mouth alike. Do NOT believe whatever information comes at you first or whatever info comes at you most often because most probably it will **not** help you and will **not** be an effective solution to the behavior issues you may be facing.

Dear Reader, I hope you can use this book as a sharp and ready sword or battle axe in the grand melee that makes up today's "dog training information and methodology."

"The difficulty lies not so much in developing new ideas as in escaping from old ones." -John Maynard Keynes

"You must unlearn what you have learned." -Yoda

Is your dog truly happy when excited? Hold it. Let's define the root word "excite."

Excite: to call to activity, to arouse (something, such as a strong emotional response) by appropriate stimuli, to energize, to produce a magnetic field in, to increase the activity of (something, like a living organism), to raise (an atomic nucleus, molecule, etc.) to a higher energy level.

The first myth we are addressing is the age-old belief that excitement somehow is the equivalent of happiness in our dogs. This is a big one. This myth even contains a few sub-myths. Such as: "vigorous tail-wagging means pure joy to our dogs." I recently read that exact quote on tail wagging online. It was in an article written by some behaviorist and was one of the top articles that came up on Google when I did a search. To say that "vigorous tail-wagging means pure joy to our dogs" is, in my professional opinion, just plain silly. I will mention here and now that we must all remember that our dogs have a real language and in real language there are always rules and exceptions to the rules. In a genuine language there is fluidity and emphasis and expression and a plethora of other wonderful things used in order to get one's point across clearly. To simply say "vigorous tail wagging means pure joy to our dogs" is foolish and oversimplified. I'm disheartened to report to you that several of the readers of this article (which was loaded with other oversimplified doggy diagnoses and behavioral mythology) bought the information wholeheartedly and said so throughout the lengthy comments section.

Did anyone who read that article stop and think that a dog could wag its tail out of nervousness? Did they consider that dogs can and sometimes do wag vigorously while attacking another dog or person? I've seen it happen! Do you see my point? THIS is one reason why I've written Dog Myths; to help clarify and **illuminate the language of dogs**, which will, in turn, help eliminate bad behavior in both dog owner and dog. This book is for everyone with a dog or pup…and, if read with an open mind, will help a very large chunk of dogs and people that are in a tremendous amount of need. Please continue reading.

At this point let me insert a few more sub-myths under the umbrella of "excitement equals happiness for our dogs." -If the dog is dancing and moving around constantly some believe that it's a sure sign of happiness. Or, -if the dog is greeting you by climbing all over you or jumping up to say "Hi" she's just happy to see you.

We have to understand a couple of things before we can move on.

1. Our dogs are socially brilliant.

2. They can and do use this social brilliance to manipulate control over their environment and the people or animals in it.

3. Dogs have a specific language based in their amazing empirical senses.

4. The order of the senses when a pup is born is critical to our human understanding of said language.

5. By and large mainstream dog obedience training and behavioral modification methods do NOT take the dog's

senses or their specific birth and developmental order into consideration.

6. What is most important to our dogs (and vital to those of us seeking relational and behavioral excellence with our dogs) is much deeper than what mainstream dog obedience training and behavior modification techniques bring to the table. How and when dogs touch or how they avoid touch, how they utilize the space in their immediate environment, their various energy levels throughout the day, and how dogs use body movement and posturing make up the bulk of their highly social language. There is a tragic disconnect when we put training above communication.

7. Unbeknownst to most dog owners: Mainstream dog trainers and behaviorists seldom help solve <u>serious</u> behavioral issues during an efficient time period because these professionals are fixated on obedience, trick-training, and giving the dog or puppy a "job to do." Tragically, they are poorly equipped on the subjects of canine communication, calmness, self-control and sociability due to their inability to see beyond the world of obedience!

Numbers 4 - 7 are the biggest dog myths in the pet industry! We will go over them.

Excitement does NOT mean your dog or pup is happy. Let me be clear, certain levels of excitement can, of course, sometimes mean that, but escalated energy levels (in the real world) are certainly not equal to happiness. A dog is <u>not</u> simply showing how happy he/she is when they raise their energy and jump on you when you arrive home every evening, despite how badly you may want to believe that. Excitement is the raising of energy, and frankly, in any canine society, that is only tolerated so much by any calm, older, social canine, be they wild or domesticated!

If a wolf pup is too excited or practices daily habits of excitement at high levels they run the risk of actually dying! They need to learn to save personal energy! Their very survival calls for self-control. Personal energy conservation is something all balanced, older canines prize. It is something almost all creatures on the planet prize! Why don't we seem to grasp this in the field of dog behavior modification and training? Why can't we understand that calmness always wins?

Here's a quick example of doggy doorway drama that is often misinterpreted as "happiness" in our dogs by the caring dog or puppy owner and certainly by the random visitor.

Examining the myth:

You arrive home after a long day at work. Fido comes flying over to you to greet you. This would be nice except for the fact that Fido is jumping, and circling, dancing, and constantly touching you with his paws, nudging you with his nose, and, on some days, even licking you or mouthing you with his teeth.

Most everyone believes Fido is just happy to see you, right? Let's bust this myth. Here's the truth of it. Fido, at this point, is simply performing a ritual. This is his habit. Every day at the same time of day in the same exact way your dog does this in the same spot (at your door). This habit is rude. <u>This habit would never last if Fido attempted it on elders from his own species</u>. Let's not anthropomorphize loads of human happiness into the equation. Let's try to see this from our dog's point of view (or, more accurately, from our dog's point of touch and smell).

Fido's keen nose has memorized your schedule and tells him, based on the slowly diminishing level of your scent throughout the home as the day wears on, that your scent is about to skyrocket in the environment again (due to your arrival home at such and such a time every day). He is also aware of your homecoming based on the light and seasons and circadian rhythms of the earth. Fido's sensitive ears, ears that hear tones 10x better than our own, have also heard your car's approach and the garage door opening and closing. By the time you enter the home his canine eyes, which excel in detecting movement because they have more rods than cones when compared to our eyes, may have already spotted your car pulling in the driveway or seen you walking toward the doorway. He is ready.

Your dog is primed for an explosion of energy. And why not? He has done this since his youth. You have enabled it. Whether you've had the world's greatest day at work or the most horrific experience - it matters not to your beloved Fido. He has already primed and begun to raise his energy levels through the use of his amazing senses and the steady and strong Monday-through-Friday habit that has taken place throughout his entire life. You **will** give him attention. He **will** jump on you. You may even encourage it a bit, too, because you might be one of the billions of people who believe this dog behavior myth that he's…just happy to see you.

You are a fool. Please don't take offense; I was a fool to believe this too, just like billions of other dog owners.

"When gossip gets old it becomes a myth." -Stanislaw Jerzylec

You see, you and I have been sold the concept that <u>over excitement means happiness to a dog</u>. An excited dog is a happy dog. A wiggling dog that is moving around nonstop is clearly just exploding with happiness, right? This propaganda has been placed before us so frequently throughout our lives that, unwittingly, we have allowed it to settle into the mind and take root. You were sold this idea and you probably never even stopped to ask if it was true or not! And here's the most sinister thing about this particular dog myth. Professionals in the dog industry continually propagate this "excitement equals happiness" myth!

A Professional Problem

Countless veterinarians encourage raised energy levels and

excitement when a pup or dog visits them. Others vets, thank God, are purposefully choosing to play it cool and are aware of the fact that calmness is a much better tool for greeting a dog or puppy especially when one is about to medically examine them.

Did you know that the majority of professional dog trainers encourage excess excitement? It is the same with dog behaviorists! This is crazy, right? I mean, aren't trainers and behaviorists the experts on dog behavior? Dog rescue groups are big fans of overexcitement also. Dog groomers, daycare and kennel owners, boarding facilities, and dog walkers propagate unbeneficial excessive excitement too; the list goes on and on! I am not attacking the industry. I am trying to revolutionize it by furthering human understanding and in this way really help the industry. There must be a change if we truly desire improved communication. We should desire that improvement because clear communication naturally leads to better behavior in our dogs. Raised energy levels and the persistent practice of excitement do not improve behavior or relationship.

"Unlearning is more difficult than learning." -English Proverb

Below is a very real-world example. Let's get out our mental microscopes as we attempt an in-depth look at excitement from a **puppy's viewpoint** for a change.

You have a new puppy. Congrats. You're immensely enjoying your little pup for the first several days. He is so cute. He is sleepy and then playful and then sleepy again. You realize you need a couple more things to aid in grooming. You decide to pick those items up and maybe a new toy at the local pet supply chain. And because you are a good dog owner, you decide to socialize your pup a little bit by bringing him along for the ride.

You enter the big store. What is the first thing that happens when the "certified" professional dog trainer sees you and discovers your new puppy? They almost always start in with human talk and salesmanship in high pitch tones. They are being friendly, no harm in that. After a moment it turns out that the human talk and high-pitched tones are soon directed at your adorable puppy. The pro trainer will often squat down and attempt to give the pup a treat. They want to show you, the owner, that they, the trainer, are friendly and real "dog lovers" and, most usually, that they can make the pup perform a "sit." They are hoping that this may win you over into taking a group class or private training session with them.

What this professional is doing <u>from a dog point of view</u> in proper canine culture is the complete and utter opposite of what ANY balanced, older, social dog would do when meeting a puppy. The trainer or behaviorist that greets your pup in this excitable way is basically causing a problem. In canine social customs they are instantly causing a problem. The professional trainer is literally committing a social faux pas in dog culture!

When the trainer raises their own excitement through high-pitched talk, petting, and directly engaging with the puppy, that is, in essence, acting more like a puppy and not at all like older dogs. What then is left for a pup to do but mirror and match the energy! The person who raises excitement at an initial greeting is NOT at all like the mother, father, or uncle or aunt dog! The person raising the energy is NOT providing the natural calmness and leadership any older, balanced dog would provide. (Is this a huge crime? No. But let's continue)

Let us continue with the example and say the trainer just greeted the pup with high-pitched talking and then bribed the pup in return for a frivolous trick. This then causes the pup to match the high-pitched tones and fawning body language coming from the dog trainer. So the pup raises its energy level. There is now <u>zero leadership</u> in the environment, especially in comparison to, say, how the greeting would have been performed if we involved any and all calmer, older, social canines!

The older social dog would provide a proper canine greeting in order to teach the puppy. At the very start the dog would provide an example of leadership. This is done through clear language. Please note, there was zero dog leadership involved in the average professional's greeting of your puppy EVEN IF THEY GOT YOUR PUPPY TO PERFORM THE SIT!

Did you know dog parents (the mother and father dog) don't care whether their pups place their butt on the ground in the sit position? That has zero to do with leadership among their species. In fact, when a dog or puppy sits this is often a poor way to greet an approaching dog because the sitter is limiting the vital information contained near the rear end. Naturally the approaching dog needs to smell their butt and genitals. We must not anthropomorphize this wonderfully unique species we call the dog.

So the ridiculous yet extremely, commonplace ritual continues on daily across our world. It happens literally EVERY day, hundreds and hundreds of times a day, across the planet. It happens in little dog boutiques and in the massive conglomerates. Nobody apparently cares to truly see what is happening. It seems in the vast majority of cases that no one ever stopped and thought about greeting from a dog or pup's point of view! So on and on and on the ugly human ritual continues and later in the pup's life, so do totally preventable behavior problems!

> **"He who won't be counseled can't be helped." - Benjamin Franklin**

Do you know who does NOT propagate this crazy yet common dog myth that "an excited dog is a happy dog"? The mother and father dog! They ignore, discourage, and, if necessary, shutdown excessive excitement. For evidence of this, simply observe dogs together at a dog park or a busy dog daycare. The parent dogs are the natural **referees of energy** levels in the dog family. If the older dogs are balanced and skilled in their own language they find peaceful ways for everyone to hang out together.

Get off the Roller Coaster before you vomit!!!

Please don't misunderstand me. Some excitement is good, and fun, and beneficial and can be fulfilling and provide a happy state of mind.

Human example: I love roller coasters! But imagine if I was stuck on the same roller coaster every day. This would lead to bizarre mental, emotional, and physical results. How is our dog's body and our dog's mental and emotional state different?

Our dogs are locked into unfortunate habits of over-excitement. These habits are totally unbeneficial and, in reality, the complete opposite of happiness! It's beyond time we got them and ourselves off this habitual roller coaster.

What used to be happiness at your doorway from puppy Fido is now just a habit of energy escalation and manipulative touch from your dog. When any dog gets to touch a person whenever, however, wherever, and at whatever energy level they want to – you can guarantee this rude touching behavior will grow into other undesirable and more serious behavior problems.

Happiness is not excitement and the practice of an overexcited state. Happiness is not just vigorous tail wagging. Happiness is not constant movement or circling. Happiness is not jumping up on you or climbing on you. Happiness is not mouthing you. Happiness is not leaning on you. These are all generally accepted dog myths that frequently lead to worse behaviors in a puppy or dog.

Happiness is...

For a super-social creature like our dogs to truly be happy takes several key ingredients. A proper relationship should be first and foremost. A healthy relationship is always the core issue. Developing healthy relationships is consistently and purposefully my underlying theme whenever I am giving a keynote, a seminar, conducting a workshop, instructing vet clinics, or working throughout my day-to-day private sessions with the dogs.

Relationship is the number one area to focus on in order to prevent, reverse, or eliminate behavior problems. This begs the question - **What is a healthy relationship to a dog?**

Is a healthy relationship one filled with bribery or payment through food? Is it one filled with punitive punishment wherein the owner seizes control of everything and micro manages the other party? Is it surface-level relating based on extreme, robotic-like obedience? Is it a relationship wherein the owner or trainer reinforces every little thing the dog or pup does? And if so, where is the maturity in that relationship? Where is the trust and the freedom in that?

Let's go further and ask - **What would a healthy relationship look like between two dogs?** What is needed for a healthy relationship between two dogs from **THEIR point of view**? What would a great relationship look like between a mother or father dog and their growing pups? What have we really observed at dog parks? How does an older, calmer dog act around a higher energy puppy? I want you to think about these questions and try to answer them for yourselves. It can lead you down a marvelous rabbit hole of canine understanding and, hopefully, far from the dog myths that beleaguer and blind masses of dog lovers. We need to ask better questions to get better answers. We need to challenge this great doggie mythology with clear observation, thinking, experimentation, and action.

Ingredients for DOG Happiness:

-Healthy Relationships: (notice relationships is plural.) Beware letting your skittish rescue dog or nervous puppy develop a fatal attraction to you. If you desire honesty and health in your relationship and the best thing for your dog, then it must not be between just you and him. In real life it is not just you and your dog against the entire world, although it may feel that way occasionally. For a truly happy dog it must not be only you, your dog, and your family versus everyone else! The idea of your family and your dog versus the world may sound romantic and make for a great novel or movie, but the reality is both parties will suffer in today's modern world. This sort of "us versus them" unsocial behavior is exceedingly common among nervous creatures and yet it is dreadfully anti-dog, and anti-healthy relationships. This sort of behavior leads to people getting bit at your front door. This sort of behavior leads to dogs attacking other dogs. It can lead to your dog getting put down.

For Healthy Relationships your dog needs:

- Exercise and Movement (fast moves) (a time for the owner to pay attention to their dog)

- Rest and Relaxation (slow or smooth moves) (a time for the owner to ignore their dog)

- Exploration (walking, hiking, going to a field or downtown in the city) (a time to explore together) (a dog uses his nose to touch and smell and taste)

- Rules and boundaries (for relationships, for exercise and playing, and for exploration)

- Leading and Following opportunities (good parenting balances both Freedom and Control)

Most dog owners do not want their lovable little pooch to be hopelessly trapped in habits of over-excitement and yet most dog owners cling tightly to this myth that excitement = happiness.

Below is an excerpt from an article I penned many years ago that was published in the Pet Connection Magazine.

Typical training uses **way too much excitement**. Please re-read that last sentence. We have been sold the concept that an excited dog is a happy dog. In many circumstances nothing could be further from the truth. When we realize that the canine uses differing levels of excitement/energy like a human uses words to communicate, we start to understand that being excited does not always mean the dog is happy. In fact, many dogs are overexcitement junkies. They are stuck in horrible habits of overexcitement because they have not been shown how to stop the addiction, or shown they have crossed a social boundary in the household. Remember, not all excitement is good. Playing ball or wrestling with your dog is good excitement. Pulling nonstop on leash or freaking out at another dog or person is not good. As humans, we get excited to go on vacation, and that's great, but we also become excited when in a war zone or if we were running from a dangerous murderer. Not all excitement means we are happy.

(For the entire article go to our blog and search the title "Calm your dog's energy and behavioral issues disappear." My blog is www.thecaninecalmer.wordpress.com If you click to Follow us that would be tremendously beneficial for you and your dog)

"Excitement is not enjoyment. In calmness lies true pleasure. The most precious wines are sipped not bolted at a swallow." – Victor Hugo

Excitement and elevated energy levels can easily lead to fight or flight displays in our dogs. And yet most forms of mainstream dog training are still engaged in pumping up the energy to produce raw obedience! **These behaviorists, trainers, and dog owners sacrifice what is most important and primary (relationships and clear communication) in order to pursue what should naturally be secondary (tricks and obedience).** They unwittingly forego healthy relationships the way any higher creature in Mother Nature would build them and the way all dogs logically build them in exchange for excitable and often frivolous tricks! They put the secondary in place of the primary. The dog, then, is just performing and working.

I don't know about you, Dear Reader, but I much prefer a relationship with my own dogs that is modeled after the dog parent and their pups than the tragically commonplace employer and employee (obedience-based only) relations many dog owners have with their dogs. **The companion housedog of today has the potential to be wonderfully social and should be different than the specialized workers our dogs were years ago**. We need to raise the bar. (We will get into this more throughout the book).

Energy control is crucial to understand if you have a dog or pup with a behavior problem. The energy needs to be calmed. **Our dogs need to learn to self-soothe if we ever hope to have real and lasting results behaviorally. Surprisingly, a great relationship and a great life with your dog, has extraordinarily little to do with excited obedience and giving the dog a "job to do."**

Mirror, Mirror in my dog

Our dogs and our puppies mirror our energy levels. They mirror our movements. They mirror our expressions. Dogs do it better than chimpanzees, dolphins, wolves, and wombats because of thousands of years of domestication. They do it so well because of proximity. A simple truth of life -Whoever we are around the most influences our behaviors the most. We pick up mannerism, ways of talking, life skills, and good or bad habits by the company we keep. Our dogs do, too.

Our dogs are what I phrase as "ultra-domesticated." It is no accident they have earned the title "man's best friend" after thousands and thousands of years partnering and living with us. They are not sleeping in the barn like the horse or cow. Our dogs are needy. Our dogs need healthy relationships with us. This is somewhat different from a cat's way of relating toward their human owner. A cat can go hunt on its own and can survive. Our dogs need us.

Almost nothing on the planet can compare to the human-dog bond in its uniqueness and closeness. Dogs have a greater understanding of human emotion, movement, expression, eye contact, body language, and social dynamics than several other creatures. They mirror us. And they have the ability to manipulate us.

Studies have shown that from an incredibly early age our puppies are social dynamos. In *The Genius of Dogs*, a book by Brian Hare and Vanessa Woods, they mention a surprising finding where young puppies with little to no exposure to human beings were nearly as skilled at comprehending human gestures as adult dogs with exposure were. This is amazing! This also is one reason why dogs can be such incredible manipulators.

Are you a Leader or a Loser? What is dog leadership?

"He who has great power should use it lightly." - Seneca

Develop your leadership skills and your dog will mirror that. It can be that simple. When one considers how dogs came into being and the specialized jobs they were bred and engineered to perform, we cannot discount the subject of relationship between leader and follower.

Good leaders are never tyrannical. If we examine history we find that tyrannical and oppressive sorts of leadership can never last. Eventually, when things get bad enough, there is a revolution.

"One of the tests of leadership is the ability to recognize a problem before it becomes an emergency." -Arnold Glasow

That quote by Glasow really resonates with me as a pro dog trainer and also as a man looking to become a better leader. When viewing the dog training and behavioral modification industry by the reading of books, the watching of dog training television shows, the searching of YouTube videos, the observing of differing dog rescue groups and veterinarians, and by seriously scrutinizing other training professionals in the field, I was astonished when I realized that these professionals were often unable to recognize the simply key problem within the dogs they were training or rehabbing! The professionals seemed to be <u>locked into a system of obedience training</u> so that they were not free enough to stop and think. The "busy work" of trick training held a blinder over their eyes and they could not look directly at the problem. Mainstream trick training and obedience training does <u>not</u> recognize and prevent behavioral problems! Fear, anxiety, and aggression can grow within a dog and people are not seeing and addressing these issues before they become an emergency. Clearly leadership and creativity was lacking in the industry. I'm sorry to say, it still is. We need a bold change. We need efficient leaders.

So let's ask. Are we good leaders for our dogs? What is natural leadership? If we <u>watch older dogs interact with younger ones</u> we can pick out several beneficial clues to these questions. It can be fun and extremely enlightening simply observing the differences in mannerisms, energy levels, and movements and postures between older dogs and younger ones. I've always found the behavior of older, calmer, balanced dogs applied towards the younger ones to be fascinating. Their leadership and example can be likened unto an illuminating lamp that reveals the best path as we travel through the dark, rough terrain of dog behavioral problems. We must cultivate a sharp eye and, in addition to that, practice smooth, efficient movement through our bodies and with our own energy when interacting with our dogs if we truly are seeking the best possible relationship and clear communication.

"Great leaders are almost always great simplifiers, who can cut through argument, debate, and doubt to offer a solution everybody can understand." -Colin Powell

Calmness is a great asset

> **"Calmness is the cradle of power." – Josiah G. Holland**

Calmness, throughout the natural world, is a treasure more valuable than diamonds or gold because it means that whatever creature finds itself in a calm state is obviously not engaged in fighting or taking flight from something! If an animal is calm they are conserving their own energy reserves. This aids greatly in survival. Calmness also aids greatly in becoming a wonderful companion in this modern world.

Calmness: the state or quality of being free from agitation or strong emotion, the state or condition of being free from disturbance or violent activity.

Did you notice the words "free" in the definitions for calmness? I love that! Good leadership and good parenting regularly evoke freedom. Being a great dog owner has much to do with freedom. Scores of us need to give our dogs more freedom. To balance that it is worth noting that many of us err and give way too much freedom and not enough boundaries. Nature calls for balance.

We cannot give total freedom where our dogs are concerned for two reasons. One big reason is that some dogs, depending on their personality type, quickly take advantage and do whatever the hell they want to do and, if left unchecked, would grow into a monstrosity. All of us, human and dog alike, are in need of a few well-defined rules and boundaries in order to have the stability and structure to navigate this world. Be sure and provide your dog these boundaries and structure if you truly care about your dog, pup, or child, for that matter.

We cannot give 100% total freedom because our dogs are domesticated and neotenous. They are permanently youngish. This means they remain somewhat juvenile due to domestication. This is what makes adult dogs more pliable and playful than the adult wolf. Neoteny makes our dogs more adaptable, trainable, respectful, and trustworthy.

"Leadership should be born out of the understanding of the needs of those who would be affected by it." - Marian Anderson

The good leader balances freedom and control. What I have observed within dog society is that the good leader gives ample freedom. In fact, I firmly believe there is more freedom offered among canine society than any human society or culture. The good leader dog allows for much trust and freedom. That is until things may be about to go in the wrong direction socially, or until the individuals in their care start raising unbeneficial energy and begin to spiral out of control. Then the good dog leader takes action and, if necessary, controls the situation as smoothly as possible until they restore a proper level of social, beneficial calmness within the offending dog's body and energy. The good leader relishes honesty in the relationship and deals directly with problems. This approach helps maintain a socially acceptable energy within all members of the family within the environment. As soon as this certain level of cohesive calmness is restored, then the good leader fades away into the background. In essence the parent or leader dog rolls back the firm, steady, calm control that they placed over the erring individual while simultaneously adding relaxation and restoring freedom and trust. Physically, they take the erring pups' space and cut off their movements. The leader does this in order to cultivate within the erring individual a moment to stop and think things over. As soon as the wayward dog or pup pauses and spatially acknowledges the parent/leader dog, it is over. The good leader then eases off and gives back the space and starts fresh with renewed trust and freedom by walking away. Then the team is able to move ever onward and upward together.

"The challenge of leadership is to be strong, but not rude; be kind, but not weak; be bold, but not bully; be thoughtful, but not lazy; be humble, but not timid; be proud, but not arrogant; have humor, but without folly." -Jim Rohn

That is how skilled, social, older dogs do it. They provide calmness through **beneficial pressure** whenever they disagree with something that is unhealthy or rude. Their conversation is based in movement and space and energy and, like a strength coach or workout buddy, they add the proper amount of pressure and tension in order to make the "muscle" grow. Most often this tension is purely psychological, though it is expressed in the environment and around the erring dog or pup's body spatially. Growth comes after the pressure, just as muscles grow if pressured correctly and then given rest and recovery. Pressure on and pressure off. That is the key for calm communication, and with repetition, eventually results in greater levels of relaxation. (For more on the application of these custom calming techniques see my upcoming book, *Talking Not Training: Forget Reinforcing your dog – Focus on Relationship*)

The dog parents are the referees of energy and the bringers of this **beneficial pressure** for total clarity in their communication whenever they see the need. They bring pressure spatially and then release it spatially. The parents address the individual and then bring greater relaxation, calmness, and then freedom. That's perfect canine conversation.

Calmness always wins. Please take a moment and think of any sports team, any boxing match or martial art, any CEO leading a company, any president or king, any good leader of men or women from the past to the present and on into the future...was calmness one of their traits? Does the top brain surgeon on the planet need calmness? Is calmness an ally for the commander of a Navy SEAL team?

Dusko Popov, Serbian double agent, part of MI6, and Ian Fleming's real life inspiration for James Bond, knew how to stay calm in life or death situations! Calmness, I'm sure, was a valuable asset for him.

Is it any different in nature? I think not. If anything a wild creature needs more calmness than our dogs because the stakes are much, much higher. If your domestic dog blows his personal energy reserve like a moron by barking and running back and forth non-stop at any person or creature that passes your fenced front yard, chances are your dog will still be provided with food, shelter, and water. If a wild wolf blows all its energy chasing a coyote off a kill, the chances of that wolf being able to hunt successfully the next evening begin to diminish. So, in a good number of cases, the wolf still may give chase to the coyote but will not chase it too far in order to intelligently govern personal energy.

Personal energy control or conservation is critically important. It is of the utmost importance if one desires a calm, wonderful household companion. The point is, domestication offers an exceedingly cozy lifestyle and that has given our dogs and pups the ability to become hyper, out of control, excitement junkies! If they were earning their keep in the wild they'd either wise up quickly or just die as fools with zero self-control. Calmness is a great asset.

The mainstream behavioral modification methods and the larger part of dog training methods across the planet go against the calm, natural way! Yes, they literally work against calmness and THIS is the single biggest reason why copious amounts of professional trainers and behaviorists do NOT actually get the fantastic results that they could be getting! I know this because our company actually achieves these amazing results when so many others do not. We succeed where they fail because we equip our clients and their dogs with calmness. We equip them with natural ways to influence energy in the dog.

Garrett's tip:

Please examine as many intelligent and social creatures as you can on this fine planet of ours. Really watch and be open to learn from a "lesser" creature. Personally, I have learned so much just by observing our dogs. They have much to teach. All the ancient wise men of the past have proverbs, writings, and fables; a host of which were gleaned from truly experiencing nature and keenly observing the amazing creatures that surrounded them.

Instead of just throwing your puppy into a group class for a few weeks because it's the normal, status quo option, or instead of just plowing forward with your personal home training by bribing the puppy with food to elicit meaningless tricks, ask yourself – what is really most important? (Please note I am for giving an occasional treat. What I am adamantly against is cultivating a philosophy and methodology where bribery with food is lauded as modern or the end-all-be-all of behavior modification. Anyone relying on some external motivator like food will never have as much success as someone utilizing internal motivation like relationship and communication.)

Or, depending on your personality type, before some of you smack your puppy around or roll it onto its back to prove you're the "alpha" please ask yourself these questions.

What would the parent dogs do? How do they successfully raise their own pups? How can you calm your pup down naturally? What is the most efficient way to achieve great results behaviorally? What motivates our pups <u>internally</u>?

Like Mark Twain said, "Whenever you find yourself on the side of the majority it is time to reform." Yes – whenever we are thinking with the status quo there is a large chance that we are not, in fact, thinking much at all. When we find ourselves in the crowd, typically we are mentally coasting. Do not settle for status quo thinking. Don't just follow the crowd. Think differently. Think like a good leader. Think like a dog.

Chapter 2 – Myth 2

-A dog is submissive when he shows his belly

"A lie can travel half way around the world while the truth is putting on its shoes." -Charles Spurgeon

You've probably lived your whole life thinking that whenever a dog or pup flops over and **exposes their belly they are being submissive or they just want a belly rub**. WRONG! If we closely observe a normal puppy and their interaction with us for a few hours of the day, one might discover how false this common myth is.

Let me clarify. Dogs have a genuine and fluid language. When a dog rolls onto their back and shows you its stomach and groin area it CAN occasionally signal submission. Let me clarify further. It is usually NOT submission when performed in front of a human! Flopping over and exposing the underside is a clear act. The dog or pup is telling you exactly how and where to pet them (manipulating spatial control and directing our touch on their body). There's nothing wrong with that if it's only done occasionally since we are trying to have a real relationship with proper give and take, but many dogs become addicted to the control. They claim their own body and tell us exactly where we can and cannot touch them! That is not good.

Another reason a puppy may flop down in front of us is to keep the rude game of mouthing going. They may have been mouthing the furniture or your shoe or nipping you and when you went to touch them in order to stop them or take them away from the area they become dead weight and begin nipping with those needle teeth. Puppies will do this over and over in attempts to get out of any sort of learning or discipline. Rude pups or dogs that don't want to listen will often go belly up when their owners go to touch them. One can witness this body language clearly whenever a flustered puppy owner tries to hold onto their pup in order to stop their nipping onslaught.

Yes, most often this rolling over and exposing the belly posture is rude and controlling in a dog-to-human display. This doesn't just apply to young dogs. This belly up body language can be manipulative even when displayed from your friendly senior dog! Because it is a real relationship and a genuine language it is possible for dogs to enjoy getting belly rubs while simultaneously gaining, in their mind, the upper hand.

As stated, exposing the underside and rolling over performed by a young puppy or unsure dog towards another dog (who speaks the same language) is much more often legitimate submission. We must remember that we are not dogs.

It is important to note that because we are dealing with a different species' language we cannot say that we know when the rule is always "I before E." Quite often in a real, fluid language there are exceptions to the rules and we have an exception here. We have in the dog language an "Except After C" phenomenon. That is one reason this dog myth is so widespread.

As I help empower our clients and translate for the dogs, I purposefully bring up this myth because it is such a smooth and easy manipulation for puppies and dogs of all ages to pull on hapless owners – and to manipulate professional vets, trainers and behaviorists too!

"And if any man think that he knoweth any thing, he knoweth nothing yet as he ought to know." -1 Corinthians 8:2

Let's be honest. We are such suckers as people, myself included. As people we are naturally arrogant. We often think we know something (especially in today's digital information age) and before hearing both sides of the story, or before wise contemplation, or proper observation or actual experimentation, many of us go shouting it from the rooftops, telling family and friends, and plastering it all over social media. This is one way that false beliefs and myths grow or, at least, continue to exist.

Manipulative Movement

Have you ever seen an MMA match? I love martial arts and boxing. I work at becoming better at them multiple times a week. Fighters use whatever advantage they can find to gain an upper hand. They want control. They seek to control the octagon/ring, to control their opponent's body, to control and impose their own will, and to get the win. I'm here to tell you that a lot of our sweet, furry friends are no different.

When we observe a martial artist stop using his stand up striking game (Muay Thai kickboxing, western boxing, etc) and then switch to wrestling or "pulling guard" in Brazilian Jujitsu; he is still looking for an edge to help him win. When the fighter switches from striking with punches and kicks and then goes for a takedown or drops to the mat in order to wrestle, no one watching in the audience that is in their right mind would say that he's giving up because he dropped to the floor. This is because he is not giving up. Instead, he is changing his strategy and altering the fight. He is moving his body into a different position in hopes of getting more control. He's probably playing to his strengths and simultaneously testing his opponent's skills.

Did you know that this is the exact same thing that happens in the bulk of cases when our dogs or puppies flop over onto the ground as we are touching them or attempting to touch them? They often become dead weight and, if the dog is hyper, or young, or rude, they will show their belly and then lick, mouth, nip, and or paw at our hands or feet. They want to control their own body and control ours while simultaneously slipping our touch or directing our touch to exactly where THEY want it! In many cases they might want us to bend over and work harder while they are comfortably flopped on the floor nipping, pawing, and spinning around. In other cases they are telling us just exactly where to pet them, and as I mentioned before, where not to pet them, which can quickly become a rude habit. And once in a while if you have a skittish pup or dog they will flop over and show you their belly, but even if it is in fact motivated by fear or submission it can STILL be quite manipulative if left unchecked! We have to be aware of our habits and our dog's habits. Let's take a closer look.

Examining the myth:

Your wonderful Labrador puppy just turned four months old. Congrats. He's now been in your household for about 2 months. That is two months as a human measures time. In a dog's reality and in a young pup's tremendously accelerated growth rate, if we were to try and compare him to how a human child develops that could, in essence, be years' worth of learning and growing! And as those days speed past, the puppy has taken an active experimentation role. Can I chew on this? Can I poop here? Where do I sleep? Can I touch you here? Is jumping up ok? Do I have to listen to you as well as to him or her? Et cetera.

You arrive home from work after a busy day and let your cute Lab pup out of his crate to go potty. After completing his business in the back yard successfully you both trot inside together. You walk into the kitchen to make yourself dinner and your pup proceeds to jump up and nip at your hands, your shoes, and the bottom of your pant legs. What is one to do?

At first you try ignoring the behavior because that's what the books said to do, right? Last month the ignoring used to work but this month he has more energy and speed and the nipping and mouthing is getting irritating. Those needle teeth of his hurt! His sharp teeth have already ripped and ruined a shirt of yours.

Next you try obedience training to stop the nipping and proceed to tell him to, "Sit." He performs it perfectly…for three seconds. Then he is back at you again - pinprick teeth leading the way. You don't want to put him back in the crate since he was in there for several hours while you were at work. The little guy needs to get his energy out. So you redirect him onto a toy. This should work since it's practically every dog behaviorist's and dog trainer's solution. This would be like giving him a little job. So you stoop down and grab one of his toys. You shake it and he stops nipping your feet to grab and tug the toy. Success! For only six seconds. As you grab some seasoning from the pantry your furry bundle of energy and teeth comes charging at you again, jumping up with renewed vigor and catching your hand with a curved, little, canine tooth. That does it!

You decide to do something a bit more direct and try to discipline the little guy by shouting, "NO!" in his direction. Your pup pauses for a moment then continues the onslaught, almost building upon the sound energy you may have just inadvertently supplied.

This time you reach down and grab a hold of his collar in an attempt to stop the steady and constant barrage of needles stabbing and scratching at your hands. (Pay attention now, Dear Reader) You caught his collar and so he decides to disagree with this by increasing his level of energy and mouthing your hand more wildly, swinging and flailing his open mouth around back and forth in an attempt to hit and strike your hands. He's figuring that this increased intensity should cause you to let him go. You decide you don't like that and since he's being such a brat you'll grab his snout with the other hand and close his mouth. It works for about one second and then…then…he becomes dead weight in your hands. While you were holding him he was steadily backing out of your hold. He flops on the kitchen floor, belly up, and paws up, and you didn't even notice that you let him go when he did it! He smoothly backed his butt away from you while swinging his teeth at you from side to side, and then he dropped the level and spun like a crocodile performing a death roll. He instinctively knew you'd have to try and stop his spinning and flopping movement (if you indeed wanted to stop the bratty puppy behavior) by bending your tall, bi-pedal human form all the way down to the floor. He's making you work harder and come down to where he is! He's employing a masterfully manipulative move that quite often ends with the owner giving up and not following through with anything. Dog 1 - Human 0. Your puppy just learned who controls touch, space, energy, and who is more persistent in the relationship. He learned that if he struggles or freaks out enough you will yield.

This was a very real example. Did it resonate with you? I hope so. Have you been in a situation like that before?

A big part of the solution would be NOT letting your puppy or dog change the level on you. <u>Don't let your dog or pup control space. Don't let your dog or pup control the touching "game."</u> You need to keep his head in the same space as when you originally grabbed his collar. To find success for the two of you, you must control the space around your own body and his little body just like his birth parents would. When harmful, rude or overboard energy and touching is rising in a puppy, the mother or father dog (or uncle or aunt or grandparent or any older social canine) would <u>switch from ignoring the behavior to addressing the behavior and it is efficiently done through spatial control and touch control.</u> As the pup shrinks his energy back to normal and acceptable social levels, the older dogs then give the pup all the freedom in the world. It is a beautiful and clear exchange that happens. Professional trainers and behaviorists need to learn this interaction. Vets need to learn this. We all need to learn these moves! What I'm describing to you goes far beyond training and behavior modification as defined in the industry today. These movements are how dogs literally speak to and manipulate people and if we can identify the spatial manipulations we can prevent rudeness and problematic behavior issues by clearly speaking the language back to them. We can build a much brighter, much calmer, much freer future for our dogs and pups and for ourselves.

Please remember, dogs have a genuine language. As stated, sometimes the flop and roll exposing of the belly is indeed a more submissive gesture. More often than not, though, it is controlling/manipulative in nature because the dog is totally determining how and where we touch them and or escaping and slipping our touch, or just plain ignoring what we are trying to talk to him about or teach him. This raises another question.

If it is in fact one of those times where the flop and belly exposure is indeed a submissive gesture toward us, why on earth would we desire to reinforce this pathetic posture? Why would we, as caring and loving pet owners, acting in a place similar to dog parents to this, our energetic fur-ball, want to encourage and reinforce such a lowly state and behavior in our young dog? It is, of course, important that our dogs learn to listen to us and to obey. But do they have to do it as sniveling weaklings rolled over on the floor? No! The correct answer is No. Keep in mind touch and body posturing is talk to a dog. Do we make our own human children bow and scrape anytime they talk with us or as they interact with us daily? No. That would be too extreme. Dogs that flop over every time someone goes to pet them are too extreme and clearly unbalanced. Our dogs (like our own human children) should NOT have to fear us and go into an excessive posture of submission in order to show respect in the relationship especially since the majority of time it is NOT submissive. But even if it was, that would not be a balanced interaction. It's a poor conversation and will not help you in building a healthy relationship based on respect, trust, and clear communication. There are much better postures available to our dogs that can show relaxation, respect, trust, and a healthy relationship.

Garrett's tip:

If you've got a flopper/spinner/belly-exposure in your home – remember, it's probably just a poor habit for the dog or pup at this point. Keep in the forefront of your mind that it is usually manipulative and is definitely a way to direct and control your touch applied on his/her body. The mother and father dog would not let them get away with controlling touch in so many interactions.

If the dog or pup flops...Stay calm. My advice – Have everyone in the household totally <u>stop petting the pooch on the belly for a month</u>. Skip all belly rubs temporarily. Initially when a flop and roll-over occurs just calmly walk away and ignore the behavior. Later, when your dog isn't as manipulative and flopping and rolling over as often, you can reintroduce an <u>occasional</u> belly rub if you so desire and if your dog enjoys it.

Addressing this dog myth and this belly issue works wonders towards a healthy relationship based on touch and space and posturing that is balanced with respect and trust through this proper handling technique.

On the other hand, if you need to address or discipline your dog or pup for doing something unbeneficial in your environment (example: your puppy is nipping or jumping up) and a flop down and belly up occurs, remember that it is an attempt by the animal to evade facing responsibility for their actions and control the space around their body. I usually advise <u>calmly pulling the dog back up into a sitting position (use their collar) and then appearing displeased on your facial expression and in your firm/serious energy</u>. Control the space around your body and theirs. Calmly keep control of the dog's head (especially if the puppy or dog is trying to mouth your hands or spin like a crocodile performing a death roll). If your hands are getting hurt from the pup's teeth do NOT let him know it! Do NOT pull back and flail your hands around in a poor attempt at getting away from the pup's snapping jaws. Instead of pulling back, reposition your hands on either side of his face while hooking his collar in order to block the mouthing with your palms. This aids in deescalating the energy after the pup's initial struggle. When employing this calming technique you are attempting to freeze your pup's head in space. This usually is best done in the sit position. You are trying to keep your pup's head still and looking up at you for a moment. This takes some sensitivity and practice. Remain calm.

What the wayward dog or pup will attempt is to create more space from you by moving their head around and snapping (side to side or backward) and wildly spinning their body around while trying to slip out of the collar. They may also attempt to climb up on you with their front paws. Or, like an ornery horse, they may try to force their face and muzzle to look straight down at the ground. Don't let any of those things happen. We are adjusting them into a relaxed yet respectful posture.

If the dog/pup remains in the sitting position without flopping down again you can smoothly release their head, calmly stand up to your full human height, and then proceed to turn your head away, then body, and walk away and ignore. Be sure that YOU walk away first. This elicits a calmer dog that is actual thinking over what just happened (and naturally this brings up their eye contact as they watch you walk away) instead of allowing the dog to manipulate spatial control and outmaneuver and out-touch you the entire time while you, the owner, get frustrated in your attempts to teach the dog/pup that you don't want a certain behavior.

An "in Touch" conversation

Social grooming and <u>who touches who</u>, and how the <u>touch</u> is applied, and when the <u>touch</u> happens determine a tremendous amount in a dog's social world and in their language. If more people knew this and discovered how to move and/or apply a calming touch on a "dog level" the world would be a far better place. If our dogs or puppies control touch, whether on our body or on their own body, one can guarantee behavioral problems will arise or are already in existence. The mother and father dog and all the uncles and aunts naturally would be able to groom the younger members of the family. The older, calmer dogs would tolerate (and ignore) plenty of touching and grooming in return from the younger members of the family until the pups crossed certain boundary lines. At this point the older and wiser dogs, the dogs that are much more skilled in canine language, would switch from ignoring to addressing the wayward pup's behavior, energy level, and movement through spatial control and touch control. The more a growing pup achieves self-control, the less their actions require direction from the parents or older dogs in the group. There are ample amounts of freedom in the canine culture so the pups can learn to make mistakes but still find a way to make good decisions.

In case you haven't noticed yet, each chapter in this book may challenge and or disrupt your old way of thinking. This should help us change how we experience our dogs' specific body language and serve to help clarify their behaviors. This is a good thing. Especially because in no other industry and with no other animal do we as people have so much differing opinion, science, personal experience, professional testimonial, and strong mythology. There is so much noise (bad info) about dogs! No other creature on the planet is as commonplace as the dog. Everyone has some form of knowledge, info, belief, or experience with or about the dog. Anthropomorphism runs amok in the dog industry.

"I can't understand why people are frightened by new ideas. I'm frightened by the old ones." -John Cage

CHAPTER 3 – MYTH 3

-If my dog is uncomfortable I should stop doing whatever is causing the discomfort

-Comforting helps soothe my fearful dog

"Nothing is more difficult than competing with a myth." – Francoise Giroud

Since we just explored the "exposed belly" myth, this is a perfect time to go a bit further into the petting, handling, and touching of man's best friend. Now is the time to look at comfort and the uncomfortable. We must examine how people handling normal dogs and nervous dogs.

A simple Google search will reveal several lame and oversimplified articles from pet professionals on how and where to touch your dog. After reading the articles you'd discover thousands of people who have also read these, wholeheartedly agree, have given positive feedback, and have devoured the mythical misinformation wholesale without the slightest inquisitive questioning as to why. So I'll ask you, Dear Reader, some questions here.

Who pays for the dog to be in your home? Who feeds and waters the dog? Who brings the dog to the vet? Who exercises the dog? Who cleans up after the dog? Who loves and gives affection to the dog? Who pets the dog and spends time with him/her? Hopefully the answer you gave is you or someone you care about that lives in your immediate household. The dog is **yours**. Your dog is NOT a wolf. The dog is **"man's best friend."** And because he's been man's best friend for thousands and thousands of years, he also has the potential to be a manipulative mastermind when it comes to human customs and the goings on in your shared environment. Man's best friend has the ability to be **"man's best manipulator!"**

Now, I know you're probably thinking, "Is he even allowed to say that about my sweet, Fluffy?" Isn't manipulative mastermind too villainesque? Are we being too hasty? I think not. In fact, I think it's a perfect description in many cases and constructively honest. An honest look helps move us forward.

We need an honest assessment of our human culture and our dogs' culture and behaviors within it now more than ever. There is a trend that glorifies our dogs and only tells one side of their story. This trend can be harmful. I have the scars to prove it! We don't like to talk about the growing number of dog bites on people. One does not often hear that the greater part of dog bites happen on our own little children and happen quite aggressively on their little faces. Casual conversation about dogs seldom includes the millions and millions of dollars spent in insurance due to dog attacks and dog bites that occur in our cities and neighborhoods each year. Those facts and figures don't make for a touching novel or screenplay. It seems we adore almost any book or movie that extols the wonderful nature of our dogs. But where are the other books about dog attacks and tragedies? Apparently they don't get published, or they do not even exist. I haven't seen any in my experience. In the very least they certainly don't garner much attention. Believe me, I have a substantial library, particularly in regard to my business, and books with detailed info on dogs and their behavior. So what gives? Why this extremely one-sided interpretation toward the animals we claim to know and love so well? One theory would be because today's culture is often all about feelings and the truth doesn't always feel good. So we lie to ourselves.

We must honestly look at any and all problems if we ever hope to find great solutions. We have to be honest in order to get real results in this life. We must seek out and look directly at the truth.

We must take a deeper look at our behavior and our dogs' behavior; an honest look. Yes, dogs have many fantastic and wonderfully noble attributes but as intelligent social creatures they also have many manipulative, bratty, and sometimes downright dangerous attributes as well. Let's get real.

"The truth does not change according to our ability to stomach it emotionally." - unknown

What I've discovered over the long and busy years working to help train people and dogs (my schedule averages 6 appointments daily and our company deals with extremely serious behavioral issues; a good number of which would easily make good television due to excessive dog drama) is that dogs are indeed master manipulators of their owners, their environment, their owners' bodies, the visitor's body, and their own furred-bodies. They are so intelligent socially and spatially, as witnessed through their little touches, that they can easily manipulate professional dog trainers and professional behaviorists and their pro training methods! They can manipulate the veterinarian and the groomer, too. We must accurately identify, read and stop the manipulations if we want to help our dogs and ourselves. We have to stop the manipulation if we want a great relationship and if we truly want less aggressive, fearful, skittish, hyper, or anxiety-riddled dogs!

<u>The myth that you should only pet your dog a certain way or only pet on certain parts of his or her body is complete hogwash. The behavioral myth that a skittish or fearful dog needs loads of human based comfort and is some how fixed through soft human talking would also fall under the hogwash category.</u> Human talking is seldom if ever the answer in the quest to calm and socialize a nervous animal.

If a dog is uncomfortable with being petted or touched a certain way guess what I have to do in my behavioral rehab work? Pet them there! If an owner comforts and coddles at the wrong time (which occurs quite often) they simply compound their own problems. It's my job to teach people and to reverse and eliminate behavioral issues. I have to begin my work wherever the animal is uncomfortable and pet them there steadily and smoothly. I hunt for ways to keep building on a foundation of respect and trust as I pet and touch the dog more and more. I then build on my touching foundation with more touching (little by little and through smooth, efficient movement) on or around the dog's uncomfortable spots or the spots on the body that the dog claims. Think of it as physical therapy, because that is exactly what it is. I am physically touching and petting, scratching and massaging areas on the dog that were previously untouchable! (Don't take this to outrageous proportions, please. It simply means if a dog isn't good with people touching his tail – I need to touch his tail. If a dog isn't good with having her nails trimmed – I touch and teach the owner how to touch her paws and trim her nails). This is crucially important in preventing, reversing and eliminating behavior problems in our dogs and pups. It all starts with proper thinking on the professional's part and that in turn should help cultivate proper thinking on the dog owner's part.

What we believe can really direct our lives to good destinations or to terrible ones. We need to clear and clean out our mind to be open to what our own dogs have to teach. Whether I'm giving a speech or working privately with a client I strive to be present and aware. I try to be focused and energetic, thoughtful yet active, and still free to be sensitive to the right messages from the dogs. Often I display purposeful insensitivity by ignoring the unsocial fears and manipulations that the dog may want to express. In this way I am clearly expressing what I want. Remember, touch and movement and energy are like words in the dog language. The dog's body always speaks. Are we listening? I learn from and listen to the dogs by closely watching their movements and sensing their energy. I highly, highly suggest we all do the same. This goes much deeper than having our dogs perform sitting, downing, staying, and other obedience. The dogs have many lessons to teach those that are willing to learn.

Unlike people, our dogs are almost always aware and present. They live in the moment. They can develop bad habits through overuse of their secondary senses (meaning they practice too much vision and too much hearing and not enough sniffing and smelling) and this always leads to trouble socially.

(For more info on that, keep a sharp eye out for my next book, *Talking Not Training: Forget Reinforcing your dog – Focus on Relationship*. I go into specifics with illustrations on The Garrett Stevens Method, our custom, natural, calming, relational rehab technique and how it is applied! We also delve deeper into all things dog language, touch, space, energy, behavior, and knowing why we must not reinforce the dog if we desire greater freedom, relaxation, and maturity in the relationship)

It is extraordinarily unhealthy for a skittish or pushy dog to control its own body and terribly unsocial to keep certain "common" areas to itself. ("common" areas being the areas on the dog's body where other dogs may want to smell or touch during play or spots on the body where visiting people may want to pat. These include almost every area on the dog's body!) **If the dog is able to control and claim certain parts of its own body, soon the dog claims more and more areas of its body and eventually they could make the jump to claiming possessions and even people in and around the home.** This behavior can quickly lead to a dangerous situation for anyone around the dog. Vets, groomers, and trainers often have to touch dogs in places where they may not like. Attention, attention: It is the owner's job to prep their puppy or dog to be physically handled everywhere by damn near everyone! That is the number one indicator of success and helps the animal achieve calmness and sociability.

I have taught seminars on dog behavior at veterinary clinics in order to equip and train their doctors and their staff. What I try to impart most emphatically is how important <u>touch and space</u> are to our dogs. **Touch is their first sense**. I instruct the veterinarians on how to stay safe from dog bites and, with our specific calming movements and methods (which are simple and direct) we are able to greatly prevent fearful reactions from their visiting dog patients. I also go over how they can prevent creating a fearful habit in their visiting patients. It is all done through touch, good timing, and communicating clearly to the dogs in a smooth, calm, and very efficient yet primal manner they can understand. Again, I cannot stress enough that, within reason, our **housedogs can and should be touched whenever and wherever a person wants to touch them!**

All this nonsense online and in books about dog handling and touching is generally backwards. Do dogs like hugs? No, typically they don't. The real question should be, do <u>we</u> like to give our dogs hugs and should our dogs tolerate and adapt to that for the sake of our relationship? YES and YES! Relationships are a two-way street. Now I'm not suggesting you go up to random dogs and pet them in weird places. Please don't go out and start a Dog Hugging Club. Do <u>not</u> teach your child to go hug the neighbor's dog. <u>What I am attempting to explain, Dear Reader, is that our dogs could be a lot more flexible, relaxed, calm, and trustworthy than they currently are across the board if we all stepped up our touch game.</u> All our dogs could be better behaved and calmer! They could be much more trustworthy. Who doesn't want that? The only way they can get there is if we learn to touch (which is talking in dog language) the right way, smoothly, and incrementally. Step by step we must lay claim socially to the dog's entire body. This is what the mother and father dogs do. **Touch and space and smell are the heart of dog language** and sociability.

"A diamond is a chunk of coal that did well under pressure." - Henry Kissinger

Examining the myth:

Many dogs in the households I visit are literally living out their lives like mini Hitlers or furry Stalins! They are living and behaving like barking and growling tyrants! I often discover that the owners encourage this behavior. Some of the time it is unknowingly encouraged. At other times the atrocious behavior is blatantly encouraged! The owners are beside themselves and emotionally exhausted. In quite a few cases the owners are also physically exhausted (or wounded) because the dog is continually outmaneuvering them physically in order to keep performing their unsocial habits. Numerous dogs are a real danger to society. Thankfully there is real help available, but only to those who can see through the dense fog of these behavioral and training myths.

The poor owners of these pushy dogs truly care about them and yet the tyrannical dogs that are living with them barely seem to give two dog turds about the relationship. It is a genuine problem millions of families face.

As we delve into our dogs' psyche and comfort levels, their likes and dislikes, and their canine preferences the truth is there for us to discover. There is a pervading belief that if our dog or pup is uncomfortable with something or afraid of something we should "stop doing that right away" and "never do what the dog isn't okay with." This belief is complete nonsense and entirely absurd! There is also a myth that every dog or pup we see in a shelter suffered tremendously atrocious abuse throughout their life and now they need extreme comfort and coddling in order to make up for their horrific past. Please beware, Dear Reader, subjective imaginations of possible past horrors, as this in no way is beneficial for helping a skittish or fearful dog move forward. Spoiling a dog can amount to a sinister and unique form of abuse!

Comfort zone versus adaptability, flexibility, sociability, and more LIFE!

> **"I try to always ensure that there are periodic moments where I do venture out of my comfort zone, because that's what keeps you alive. That's what keeps you from getting stale." -Queen Rania of Jordan**

> **"A ship in a harbor is safe, but that is not what ships are for." - John A Shedd**

A dog or puppy hiding in our arms, or lap, or sitting on our feet in order to hide its rear from being smelled and social with other dogs may seem to need comfort from us in that moment, but that is the worst possible thing we could do. A dog hiding its butt in our personal space while facing their weapons (teeth and muzzle) directly at our visiting guest does **not** need comfort either. They need an adjustment.

Dogs are extremely social creatures. At least, they are supposed to be! The balanced, normal, domesticated dog is so wonderfully social and adaptable; in fact, they can live and work with different species. Almost all animals on the planet live near other species. Few large animals, though, live right with other species in the same exact den and sleeping space as closely as dogs do with people. This amazing adaptability is something to treasure and encourage in our dogs and puppies. (Please note that the encouragement I'm talking about is seldom if ever accomplished by human talking.) This awesome social adaptability that our puppies come equipped with due to domestication is certainly NEVER helped along by comforting and coddling our dogs when they are fearful or anxious. **Never comfort when they are in a fearful or unsure state of mind and presenting a fearful or skittish body posture.** Instead, adjust them physically into a more relaxed and confident posture and don't let them hide their rear end in your personal space.

My friend, Robin Sharma, best-selling author and speaker, says, "Most people live within the confines of their comfort zone. The best thing you can do for yourself is regularly move beyond it. This is the way to lasting personal mastery and to realize the true potential of your human endowments." This same principle should apply to our dogs! What of their "endowments" eh? It should apply to them and probably would but for the many myths that beleaguer our thinking and actions toward our own dogs. We all are desperately in need of healthier handling skills and comfort zone expansion skills for our dogs.

Exercise is healthy, right?

What is exercise exactly? It is the addition of certain pressures, weights, stresses, discomforts, and movements performed or done on purpose to remove negative pressures, weights, stresses, and discomforts! We add one and we subtract another. Simple and balanced.

My friend Robin has another couple of quotes I'd like to share with you. "Your greatest growth and progress lies in the area of your greatest discomfort." Isn't that good? Discomfort can create incredible things. Discomfort and pressure turns coal into diamonds. Here's another from Robin, "Life is like working out. There's no pain in the comfort zone. But is that really where you want to live?"

"No pain - no gain" is a common expression used in the world of exercise and working out. But the intelligent implication is that the "pain" is good pain. The pain is beneficial because it is a pain that leads to greater capacity and strength. It's not actually hurting us but helping. If we simply stop doing whatever it is our fearful dogs are uncomfortable with, they will quickly draw a comfort zone around themselves blocking any and all future interactions with that uncomfortable stimulus – be it being socially normal with another dog, or greeting a visitor at the door, or being near a new baby, or the mailman, or shiny floors, or stairways, or vacuums, or motorcycles, or July 4th celebrations, et cetera!

Soon the fear that started out as a little seedling in your pup's mind has grown into a foreboding forest of horrifying habits! And you were there the entire time as the days turned into weeks and the months turned into years. Worse still, most of you inadvertently added seeds of fear by the addition of human comfort while your dog was presenting a fearful state. **Soft talk and saying, "It's OK" to a nervous or fearful dog is one of the worst mistakes we can commit on our dog's psyche and on our relationship! Never coddle or comfort a skittish dog or you will simply add fuel to the fire. A dog is not a person. By talking softly or allowing the nervous dog to always remain in your spatial bubble you will literally be encouraging and praising your dog or pup for their fearful state of mind. You will be enabling a skittish and manipulative body language.** Soon the dog can make the transition to tyrant through their nervous habits and your own inadvertent reinforcement. Soon, life is lackluster for both man and beast because the decisions are made by the pet's growing fear within the home, at the park, on the leash, and most definitely inside your own personal space!

Garrett's tip:

If the dog already has existing behavioral issues, please remember; the magic of proper touch and spatial control happens outside of the dog's small comfort zone. We can rapidly help them open up to a more relaxed life through more touching and socialization **if we know how to apply the touching and how to prevent their touching us back rudely! We must also not let them slip or avoid our touch with a form of manipulative doggy one-up.**

Did you know that all our dogs and pups are quite skilled in getting the "last word" in the conversation? This means they frequently get the <u>last touch</u> on our body or they frequently leave our personal spatial bubble before we leave theirs and in this way <u>they end the conversation in a rude manner</u>. They know what they are doing!

Watch and learn from the dogs and you'll start understanding and eventually speaking some of their language, unless, of course, you are too fixated on training the old "sit, down, stay, leave it, and come." If your emphasis is solely on their obedience training or strictly on working the dog and NOT on their actual language you'll no doubt get them to perform some tricks and commands adequately. <u>And they'll **still be able to manipulate you**</u>! Unfortunately some dogs will retain a bratty demeanor, some even cultivate greater levels of aggression, fear, anxiety, hyperactivity or other misbehaviors because all you did was <u>ADD obedience</u>. You did **not** <u>SUBTRACT poor behavior</u>. <u>This truth is evidenced in many a professionally-trained working dog that manifests problematic behaviors while easily maintaining the ability to perform great obedience in their work</u>. In my experience, dogs that have professional, advanced "obedience training" can be difficult cases to calm down! Even if the trained dog knows heaps of commands and can admirably perform the obedience rituals and do all the tricks; the animal still can suffer with serious fear, aggression, or a myriad of other behavioral issues internally. This is because obedience training is surface level and canine relationship and communication is something altogether deeper.

We must delve deeper. We must look internally at ourselves first, and then at our pets. Then, and only then, will we be truly able to learn from the dogs. In this way one can literally have the best of both worlds (internal and external motivation) (calm communication and healthy relationships with great obedience following).

CHAPTER 4 – MYTH 4

-Dog licking is the same as human kissing

-My new rescue dog is a "Real Lover"

"Touch comes before sight, before speech. It is the first language, and the last. And it always tells the truth." – Margaret Atwood

This next myth is another big one. It is the preposterous belief that **when a dog licks us it is like a human's kiss.** This is the overwhelming mythological belief that our dog is just licking us out of pure affection. It is the idea that when a dog licks us it is the human equivalent of a person kissing us.

Do our dogs make out with each other? Do dogs kiss at the end of their wedding ceremonies? Do they French kiss? I'll let you intelligently puzzle those answers out.

Dogs will lick to get more detailed information into their gustatory and olfactory senses. They will lick in order to socially groom or clean one another. They will lick occasionally to connect with a friend. They often lick out of anxiety and obsession. They will lick to claim one another, to seize space, and to one-up the other by controlling the first or last touch!

What is the first thing the mother dog does when her pups are born? Licks them to clean them, yes, but also to stimulate the nether regions for bowel movements, and to socially claim them. Their little bodies are hers!

When petting your pet and your pet gets set to pet you back, do not yet let them pet or you'll get... a manipulative pet. Say that five times fast. Just having a bit of fun. But seriously, you do need to pay attention to the crucial and life-changing information we are going over here.

We need to claim our dogs and not the other way round. The mother and father dog socially come into the growing pups' "personal" space any time they want to and groom, smell, and touch whenever they see fit. It is NOT the other way round. As the puppies grow they are taught by all older members of the family that they need to observe certain greeting rituals and specific energy levels. These things are crucial for understanding and clear communication.

In dog culture the new pup does not have "personal space." There is no such thing. The parent dogs enter their space whenever they wish. If we imagine for a moment being born blind and deaf and having multiple siblings crawling all over us we can glimpse the totally different existence dogs and pups have. This is much different than our human experience. Imagine cuddling together; crawling and laying on top of one another for warmth and connection. Imagine huddling together for basic survival from the moment you are born. The concept of privacy and personal space does not exist to the new pup. How could it?

There are also no "private parts" in dog culture because they are animals. Dogs are naked. Dogs use the areas we would label "private" in the human species, for smelling, tasting, and touching to fully gather information and to converse. What we consider private and personal is often the first thing a healthy social dog needs to investigate upon introduction to another dog. Beware of denying your puppy or dog a normal social interaction based in their primary senses of touch, smell, and taste. Beware of denying your pet a doggy "handshake." Do that too many times and they quickly can become unsocial.

Touching and grooming largely determine communication and

define who is who within a dog's family group. Maybe you've heard of how chimps, baboons and other primates groom one another to establish bonds and how this behavior pertains to their social status. Well, it's not just for primates. Our dogs touch and groom one another. Sometimes they deny another's touch on their bodies as well. This reveals so much to anyone looking to learn more about dog communication and the interspecies communication they use with us.

Often one can witness older, calmer, more social dogs put up with a lot of crap from young, hyper pups. Look closer and you'll notice these older dogs are trying to <u>ignore</u> the young whipper-snappers. And when and if the younger, less socially-skilled pups go too far, or nip too hard, or lick too much, or take up a rude body position, the socially-adept dog will quickly and efficiently <u>switch from ignoring to addressing</u> the situation in whatever way is most favorable to both parties. The communication the older social dogs provide their young is crystal clear.

If you want to raise an excellent dog and develop a wonderful, almost parental bond (very different from the common employer – employee bond most folks inadvertently end up with through the dreadfully common training techniques taught to the masses) then I would highly suggest you take a page out of the older social dog's repertoire.

The domesticated dog should not have personal space or privacy that is kept from a person. The domesticated dog is living among us in our homes. We lead them like we are parents because they are permanently neotenous. This means that they will never mature to the level of a wild wolf that makes his or her own decisions. This is a fine thing, because domestication can serve to take the cares off our dog's shoulders. The docile, domesticated pet, in turn, should be able to relax.

Ideally, today's housedogs should be able to achieve greater levels of docility, flexibility, and adaptability in their interspecies communication and as they interact socially with us and with each other. The use of fight or flight should be extremely rare in our dogs because of the peaceable way many Westerners live. If raised correctly, our dogs could learn to utilize more peaceful means of expression toward those in their environment. Is this the case or are we viewing today's dogs and their handling and training like it was 100 or a 1000 years ago?

Bottom line: Pay attention to who is touching whom and how that touch is happening. Dog licks can be quite quick. Like a skilled boxer working his jab that hits then is away before the opponent has reacted, don't let your dog manipulate you with a fast moving tongue or any other part of their body.

Examining the myth:

Let's say you just adopted a rescue dog, an adorable blue female Pit bull. You don't know hardly anything about the dog's past.

What we do know is that during the "honeymoon period" (the first two to three weeks any dog is introduced to a new location) your new gal is going to be conducting plenty of experiments. Space and touch are up for grabs in her mind's eye. If you give her an inch she most likely will take a mile or more.

Let's say that the honeymoon period goes by quickly for you and is seemingly uneventful. During these initial weeks she was sweet as ever and you both bonded rather strongly. She was always kissing you whenever you touched her and sometimes even when you didn't. But then, shock of all shocks, during the second month that she was with you she lunged for a visitor! What the heck happened to your sweet gal?

Like being interviewed by the news after your neighbor turned out to be the serial killer, you think to yourself, "She seemed fine. She was always pretty quiet and kept to herself." Or, in reality, did she keep near you? Was she in your personal space repeatedly? Was she licking you? Was she always asking/demanding attention and petting? Didn't you recently have a conversation over the phone with your mother and weren't you just mentioning to her that your new Rescue was so sweet and "such a lover" who always wants to be in your lap?

Your new rescue dog was manipulating you and probably suffers with underlying fear issues. Your new rescue very subtly began turning that fear into some aggression. You didn't notice during the honeymoon period because you thought that her licking and constant touching meant kisses and affection, affection, affection. You, like millions of others, believed the myth that a dog licking you is the human equivalent of kissing. The wild thing is, as mentioned before, it can sometimes mean that and yet it can also mean in dreadfully clear dog language "I control what I repeatedly touch!"

This is real dog speak we are talking about. Your Pit was most likely uncomfortable and nervous when the visitor tried to enter your home or tried to leave it. The point is that the dog is skittish and has manipulated the environment, your personal space, and your own body to remain fearful (or worse –grow more fearful). The fearful dog is the most manipulative creature on the planet. They are like drug addicts and fear is how they get their fix.

We get several calls, texts, and emails every day concerning dog behavioral problems and whenever the client on the phone mentions the dog is a "real lover" or "loves being in my lap" or is "always giving kisses" we know what to expect before we ever meet the dog. I expect to find a controlling, somewhat bratty, yet fearful animal desperately looking to be calmly led into a better life. And, thank God, we are able to legitimately provide excellent, real help through our specific natural methods that happily go against the status quos training methods and these numerous dog myths.

Relational Rehab:

The Garrett Stevens Method

The help we provide is <u>NOT based on bribery with food</u> and <u>NOT based on harsh handling techniques</u> (both of which are external motivators) and certainly NOT based on excitement. Our custom method is NOT even based on obedience training! Our specific methods instead are based on how dogs actually think, move, touch, smell, taste, see, hear, and raise or lower their energy in their immediate environment. Our methodology comes from the natural ways of the mother and father dog. We teach real-world leadership skills. We teach intelligent observation. We teach honesty. We teach energy control, conflict resolution, stress management, and how to calm difficult situations. We teach the art of movement. We teach healthy relationships. We teach real life skills and proven success principles to our clients and their dogs.

As the years go by and I equip, educate, and empower others, the dogs continue to educate and equip me. I am so grateful to be a part of their world and this amazing life. Are you learning from your dog?

Garrett's tip:

Whenever you go to touch a dog, if they intercept your hand with a lick, or mouth, or with their nose, or if they somehow touch you back - that is usually a sign of a misaligned relationship! It is a particularly clear sign if it happens repeatedly. This is so common. And because it is so exceedingly common means that it is not so great. Do you want a common relationship or a great one? Do you want to have a common day today or a great day? Do you want a common, manipulative dog, or a great one? The choice is yours.

What I suggest to all our clients is to win the game of touch. Whenever a dog or pup tries to intercept a friendly pat or touch from a person through excessive licking, nosing, jumping up, or mouthing, we must calmly attempt to touch first. This means don't let the dog intercept your hand while your hand is on the way to the dog's head or body. If you go to pet the top of a dog's head and they raise their energy and intercept your hand by lifting their nose and tongue, do NOT let them. Do not let them lick you repeatedly. Do not let them intercept your hand and touch your hand. You need to be the source of calmness, the controller of touch, and the chief groomer.

If you went to pet them and they cut you off, in attempts to control the conversation in dog touch, you need to adjust the conversation to a more polite and refined talk. Adjusting the dog's head position and not allowing licking or mouthing will turn rude talk into well-mannered conversation between you and your pet.

Many dogs and pups demand the "first word" in dog conversation (the interception by touching or licking) and then they demand the "last word" (they touch you last as you go to bring your hand back from their face.) Identify this honestly for what it is please. It is not affection! It is rude behavior! Don't let your dog or puppy continuously get the first and or the last touch on you because they will set the tone for a bad relationship!

"Man's mind, once stretched by a new idea, never regains its original dimensions." -Oliver Wendell Holmes Sr.

CHAPTER 5 – MYTH 5

-My dog is protecting me

"A wise man makes his own decisions, an ignorant man follows the public opinion." -Grantland Rice

-A note from the author-

(If you've read this far, then please realize you are now way ahead of the game. Congratulations. You are now a part of a potential future. So many are living in the Stone Age as far as their personal philosophy on dogs, their behaviors and training techniques, and their views on canine communication. You and I, with each chapter covered and with each myth exposed, are trailblazing the future! Please join me on the wagon, man the shotgun, and keep a sharp eye on this new, bright horizon.)

Here we scrutinize another classic dog myth. This is the false belief wherein the dog owner assumes their fearful, skittish, or out-of-control dog is a "protective" dog. A great number of people believe their nervous dogs are loyal guardians. Others believe that the fearful dominance and aggression that their dog displays is somehow an "alpha" dog personality trait. In essence, what they have is a fearful and unsocial creature that's manipulating the dickens out of them, controlling the space in the environment, and is locked into habits of rudely threatening people, other dogs, or both.

These aggressive dogs always stare directly at the guest. These dogs will growl, lunge, and make a scene all while keeping their backside safely in the unwitting owner's personal space. These dogs will threaten friends, neighbors, and many times even family members, sometimes even the dog owner's own spouse or children! These fearful and aggressive dogs may eventually bite someone. This needs to be addressed properly and I've discovered time and again that positive-only reinforcement and punitive reinforcement are NOT the most effective ways to do it!

A fearful state of mind practiced at the wrong times is a terrible thing for man or beast. Fear, if irrational - and a multitude of fears are - can creep into the mind like a noxious weed and quickly form a chokehold on one's decisions. As my friend Robin Sharma says, "The fears we don't face become our limits. The opportunities we don't seize become our walls."

Are you filled with fear? Is your dog filled with fear? How often is fear rearing its ugly (and addictive) head in your puppy or dog's life? In my day-to-day experience successfully rehabbing serious aggression in dogs, even in dogs that have killed other dogs or attacked and bit people, I would estimate 95% of the aggressive cases we see are fear-based.

Are you identifying the fear in your "protective dog" and addressing it properly? There is a HUUUUUUUUUUUGE chance you are NOT dealing with the fear and aggression properly. This is because there is also a huge chance the professional dog behaviorist/trainer you hired is NOT dealing with it properly or naturally either! First of all, the majority of professionals concern themselves with making our dogs work and perform obedience. In reality, that has little to do with fear or aggression or anything internal or psychological, for that matter. Secondly, the professional is still mentally surrounded by these dog myths and probably even subscribes to and propagates some of them. And lastly, people often have trouble dealing with dog fear and aggression because of the differences found in our two species! Let's take a closer look.

As human beings we tend to mishandle fear in our own lives quite frequently. As people attempting to fix, modify, address, correct, or help remove, prevent, or reverse fears in a dog, it's an even greater failure. We fail to properly address fear in our dogs time and again. Why? Here are some reasons why people in general are terrible at helping fearful dogs and fixing aggression in our dogs despite loving them so much.

Examining the myth:

<u>What NOT to do…</u>

1. We softly say, "It's Okay." And we say it repeatedly!

Think with me for a moment please…at surface level you are literally telling your dog that their fearful state of mind is "Okay!" <u>You are literally telling your dog that it's okay to threaten the guest attempting to walk in your front door</u>! For pup's sake - Please stop doing this! Please consider spreading the word about this excellent book or at least what you've gleaned from it about stopping fear. You'll really help the world a bit and you'll most definitely help your dog or someone else's and you could potentially help the terrified visitor attempting to come in the home.

Why do we attempt to sell our dogs out of their fears with human talking? We talk softly and try and sell them verbally because we are human. At this point all of us in developing or developed nations all over the world are quite disconnected to the natural world. We are disconnected from our dog's super senses. We are no longer Tarzan or Mowgli. We are basically thermostat crankin', bed sleepin', skinny jean wearin', car drivin', TV watchin', fast food eatin', selfie takin', social media driven', internet addicted people of today. There's not a legitimate Crocodile Dundee in sight, despite what is portrayed on "reality" TV programming. We, as modern folk, have blunted senses. Dogs are different. Dogs are still connected to the wild by their highly-developed senses.

This human coddling and soft-talk is so stinking common and yet so debilitating to dogs and puppies because we are actually working 100% against Mother Nature! By attempting to comfort the weak-minded dog that presents a psychologically fearful state with soft, baby-talking, and human salesmanship, and by allowing them unlimited access into our personal space, we only condition the dog further into their shrinking comfort zone or fearful state of mind.

This happens so often because we fail to realize what is actually occurring in our dogs and in their exceptionally perceptive senses during moments of fear. We keep addressing their ears by talking when the fearful dog is already over-using their eyes and ears to ramp up the energy in their fearful and aggressive state. The nervous dog then proceeds to threaten the neighbor with everything that is in them. They easily outmaneuver us, point their muzzle (weapons/teeth) in a direct line at the neighbor and bark and lunge! We coddle them and almost praise them softly for doing it!

Please, please, please disagree with fear in your own life and in your dog's when you find it. Don't say, "It's ok" or "you're fine" softly to any dog while the dog is losing its mind and freaking out on someone or something again! Also, I think this is worth noting, if it was legitimately "okay" and everything was in fact normal, then there would be zero need to keep saying "it's okay" over and over and over. You're not fooling anybody by talking. It is far, far better to do almost anything else rather than coddle or run our mouths at that critical moment. (This is brutally honest info – I realize – but bear with me because I'm writing it to help you and help the dogs we all love)

2. We let them take physical and spatial control and put on a big production.

Instead of talking with our mouths, we should "talk" with our body and the space around our body and direct the space around the dog's body. Dogs are faster than us. It is a fact. Dogs are usually more skilled in movement than us. Don't be discouraged. Our dogs should be better movers than us since that is their main language. Keep in mind the dog language is all about touch, space, body movements and postures. Remember, touch is their first sense! Space in the environment is critically important for influencing behaviors. Do not let them outmaneuver you.

Never let your fearful dog "protect you" against a visiting relative or guest. This is accomplished by controlling your dog's movements <u>before</u> they ramp up to outrageous levels. This means intercept your dog's body and eye contact early and control the space in front of you and in front of them. NEVER let your "protective" nervous dog place its rear end in your space and threaten anyone. That is only more proof that the animal is fearful and manipulating you! Do not let them position themselves in front of you, weapons pointed at the friendly relative or guest all while their butt is positioned so you are seemingly protecting and watching their "six." In military terms your six is your backside. Don't protect their rear end. Expose it!

<u>Cultivate a good heel</u> so the dog can learn <u>leash manners without pulling</u> (pulling escalates energy). This way the dog never ends up way in front on your walks. We don't want the dog in front, staring and snarling while poor pathetic you are stuck behind them. You must stop your own dog as he/she stares at, barks at, lunges at, and/or goes after the guest at your door or person on the street. You must stop your dog from manipulating you spatially! They will use any tension on the leash to escalate their energy. So make a quick tug then make sure the leash goes slack and keep them by your side. Don't let your dog be in front of you or hiding behind you as both positions could be attempts to control the situation in an unsocial way. You must be astute and aware of the dog's attempts to use your space to gain power to threaten and stare at the guest or stranger or random dog. We must actively disagree (just firm enough to control the space in the environment and the dog's body). Then we must calmly give back some space to our dog. Be aware of your dog and their attempts at teaming up (their

body with yours) in order to bully or threaten someone or something. The skittish dog will always try and use the dog owner's body and personal space to cover their vulnerable backside.

Garrett's tip:

Never give Comfort when you should provide Conflict. Here we get to the root problem for many people. A great many people have a fear of conflict. We need to realize dogs are honest animals. We need to realize conflict and disagreement can be amazingly beneficial in our lives and in the life of a wayward dog. Does this mean we abuse or mishandle the animal or the situation? Certainly not. Does this mean we are FREE to disagree? YES! Never comfort when conflict should naturally occur. This may be surprising and shocking, I know, but conflict can be great if brought about clearly, smoothly, spatially, and ended favorably. Think of it like disagreeing and having an honest and beneficial talk with your child or teenager.

A great deal depends on the nature of the dog owner and their personality type when attempts are made to apply this calming beneficial conflict technique. When people attempt to bring a resolution by addressing their dog's improper behavior, the majority of folks fall into two categories of failure and poor results.

Group 1

The first group doesn't bring enough firm energy and fortitude to the table. They are super friendly and sweet in their attitude while they are disagreeing with their dog. This will not work. This will not work in the midst of a doggy manipulation. The dog sees right through them. Or, to put it precisely, the dog doesn't even see them because the person's energy is too sweet or too low to even register in the dog's mind at that particular moment. So the animal looks right past the owner in order to bark or lunge at whatever stimuli they are fixating on. The misbehaving dog, in essence, is blowing their owner's weak energy/low energy levels out of the water and thus proceeds on unabridged with their own fixation, high energy, and bad behavior. <u>This poor behavior characteristically presents itself in some form of extreme fixation almost always initiated by way of the animal's secondary senses (vision or hearing)</u>.

We need to consider the dog's energy and <u>our own energy</u> at the moment. We need to consider the dog's body and <u>our body</u> at that moment.

Quick example: Level 1 is the calmest energy level and level 10 is the highest (total fight and flight explosion). Creatures naturally move up and down on this energy scale throughout their day depending on several factors. The question is what levels of energy are we practicing? Are our dogs mirroring those? Are our dogs practicing beneficial energy levels or are they addicted to wasteful, too high energy levels?

It is impossible for a creature with an escalated energy level of 5 to ever listen to, or respond appropriately, to anyone attempting to get their attention and converse with them through movement at an energy level of 4. This is because 4 is less than 5. A level 4 energy is calmer than a level 5. The 5 cannot or will not deescalate for a level 4. It is impossible.

The name of the game is to **match the energy level** of the dog **then induce relaxation!** If you are skilled in the ways of dog movement and body language, and match your dog at the earliest possible outset, like a 1 or 2 energy level, things go quite smoothly for both you and the dog. If you efficiently address any behavioral issue spatially and bring a steady, calmer, yet firm disagreement to your dog at the earliest possible moment, the dog can calm down much, much quicker. <u>Use the leash if necessary</u>. <u>Step into your dog's space and back them up so they cannot come forward</u> at the guest or the dog they are attempting to threaten or attack or the doorway they are attempting to escape through. Make your body bigger. Expand and take up space. Bring firm energy and a serious countenance. Bring patience, too. Above all, bring persistence because dogs as a whole are more persistent than modern people.

We need to cultivate this skill of <u>disagreeing with our dogs peaceably</u> and smoothly and leave them better for it. The parent dogs are exceptional at this. Many older, balanced dogs can be tremendously beneficial examples for dog owners desirous of behavioral change. They are examples to how we, as people, could bring a bit of <u>valuable conflict</u> to the rude or rebellious dog or puppy until the dog deescalates his energy to an acceptable social level and is polite again, respectful and trustworthy.

Calm yet firm spatial control all while matching and then deescalating the energy is the name of the game. But for those certain personalities that have trouble being firm, it will simply not work. It is the same as parenting our human children when they have misbehaved – we need beneficial and appropriate levels of firmness in the conversation. When it's time to get serious you must be serious.

Group 2

Let us not forget the other group of people and their personalities when examining this constructive and calming conflict and how our dogs benefit from it IF performed properly. The other type of personalities we find are the ones that may be inclined to control or dominate the dog. These folks often err through over-correction. Or they err in their definition of what a "correction" is or how a correction is applied. Several of them still believe the old school training beliefs that a correction is simply when you yank on a dog's leash, hang a dog, or roll it over onto its back. I don't condone or suggest those methods. This type of person would typically bring a level 8 energy (from themselves) to a wayward dog that was only at a level 5. If this resonates more with you and your personality type, then proceed with caution, because overdoing it emotionally or physically like that can create fear in the dog that <u>the owner falsely interprets as respect</u>. If you're overboard you could unintentionally raise fear and aggression. We must be physical because we are attempting to speak dog just as one must be physical when speaking in sign language. We must never be brutal or domineering. Remember, dogs speak through movement, touch, energy, and the space around their body and environment.

Our specific conflict technique (the Garrett Stevens method) is <u>based in calmness</u> and, if done properly,<u> brings about **greater calmness, understanding, and a healthier relationship resulting in both trust and respect due to the clear communication applied spatially**</u>. More freedom is soon had by all species involved! Greater relaxation and trust can be yours and your pets!

The goal is to match certain movements and to match the energy level extremely <u>early</u> so you and your dog are on the same exact wavelength. That is clear communication done the canine way. If you match them successfully and have controlled the space around your body, your dog's body, the guest's body, and the doorway, you can then cut back on a lot of drama. De-escalation is the key. But that may require you raise your energy initially in order to match the dog's. You want to accurately match their energy and take their space so they look up at you for a moment and not the stimuli. That may require some initial drama from you. It's ok to mirror the dog's behavior back onto them a little so they can recognize what they are doing is unwanted.

This, Dear Reader, is the A, B, Cs of dog language. When we first learned our A, B, Cs there was some drama involved. There was a song with a certain rhythm. In some kindergarten classrooms the A, B, Cs are displayed in vivid colors and cartoons on the walls. This is drama. Drama helps the brain remember. Utilize drama to match the dog's energy if necessary. Use calmness and firmness and patience applied spatially, for those are the key ingredients to lead your dog into a healthy relationship AND great behavior, too. Do not pay the dog to look at you as this has little to do with dog language or respect. Relationship and communication comes first. Your dog will thank you!

(For more info and illustrations on applying Garrett Stevens' custom caring, calming, conflict technique please refer to my next book.)

CHAPTER 6 – MYTH 6

-I can love this rescue dog and fix all the problems

-Human love and affection alone can modify dog behavior

"Care and responsibility are constituent elements of love, but without respect for and knowledge of the beloved person, love deteriorates into domination and possessiveness." - Erich Fromm

Human love and affection is a wonderful thing. And one might argue that it can indeed right all wrongs and fix the problems we face in the world as people. But we need to remember that love and affection from us toward our dogs is <u>just one ingredient</u> in developing a successful relationship. Yes, Dear Reader, I agree with you, it is the best ingredient. Yes, again, I agree, it *can* help fix certain things in a dog. But, did you know human love and affection misdirected towards our dogs could also <u>hurt</u> the dog? (Insert dramatic GASP here!)

Were you aware that human love and compassion when misguided is responsible for, in my professional opinion, something akin to psychologically abusing our dogs? (Insert even more dramatic GASP here!!) That's a wild claim, right? Let's take a look at the evidence.

Dog Rescue Groups:

Thank the good Lord for quality dog rescue groups and all the fine work they are doing. Thank the Almighty again for all the thousands upon thousands of volunteers that help out in rescue. Rescuing dogs (or any animal or person for that matter) is certainly a tremendously noble task. I commend you all.

As I stated before, <u>human love and affection is only one ingredient among several</u> to be diced and dropped into the soup that leads to relational and behavioral success. If we desire the formation of excellent communication and a unique bond between owner and companion dog, yes, it begins with love, but it must not stop there. Success requires other ingredients. We must put other great ingredients into the soup. When we add the proper ingredients, this, in turn, leads to an amazing, social dog without behavioral problems.

There needs to be other components to the relationship for real success, folks. Here's a wild truth…the rescue dog does **not** need more sweaters. They typically do not need more plush and fluffy toys. The rescue dog is not in need of loads of food treats. They don't need more bows in their hair or more bandanas around their necks. The rescue dog does **not** need more excitable praise and high-pitched human talking, even though we, as people, still get a kick out of raising a dog's energy levels (no matter how problematic the result is!). We want to comfort the weak rescue dog, which is an excellent human quality that, behaviorally speaking, consistently gets us into psychological trouble with our dogs. We often allow the rescue dog free and unadulterated access into our personal space. We want to see the excited response.

Contrary to popular belief - <u>The rescue dog doesn't need someone to fawn over it</u>! But what do we as loving, caring people do? We fawn. We praise and we over-excite. We often give what dogs, if roles were reversed, would never do or give. We give what they would consider an inconceivable amount of treats. Like a cliché story about a deadbeat dad who's been cut off from his children and is later reunited – the rescue volunteer and or rescue dog adopter provides an extraordinary amount of toys and treats and praise; akin to buying or bribing one's way into a child or a dog's heart. In reality, this behavior of ours is <u>unhealthy for the</u>

73

relationship!

We must think more like dogs if we really want to help them! I suppose it's not so crazy how often we screw our dogs up behaviorally because the evidence points to how much we are screwed up as people! The new rescue dog does NOT need all that surface level crap I just described and deep down I think the better part of us know that. Instead of fluff and shallowness, our dogs need what anyone needs to have a healthy relationship and healthy life habits.

Communication, love, respect, trust, play, and enjoyment combined with a few boundaries are what any dog, or person, for that matter, in a healthy relationship needs for success. I'm sure most of you are saying, yes, of course, and yet there is little follow through when it comes to applying this communication, these boundaries, this trust and respect in a clear way dogs can understand. There is even less involvement when it comes to people learning the dog language. How can we love our dogs when we aren't even on speaking terms? Communication comes first!

I'm here to announce to the world that "modern" training isn't up to par on interspecies communication. Dogs are constantly manipulating people and our mainstream behavior modification methods because we keep relating to them at this shallow, surface level. We are not "reading dog" accurately enough and we are not "speaking dog" fluently enough.

We need to acknowledge what a healthy relationship based on canine communication, love, respect, trust, boundaries, play, and proper energy levels look like in a dog's world. I hate to break it to you but a cutesy doggy Halloween costume has got nothing to do with it!

When a physically and often psychologically wounded dog lands in the wide world of dog rescue here is often what happens once they enter an adopter's home from **a canine perspective**.

Examining the myth:

Rover's Journal.

Day 1

Where the heck am I? The place smells pretty good. These tall, two-legged creatures sure do make a lot of noise. Sound is consistently pouring from their mouths or the strange devices that surround their habitat! They keep looking at me and making more sounds. They move and touch awkwardly. So far I've been given free access to go everywhere they go in their territory. They are giving me loads of treats. I may become fat.

Day 2

They are watching me constantly and giving me loads of attention, strange, I don't recall Mom or Dad ever doing that. They let me touch and groom them anytime I want. That's also very strange. They must be looking to me for direction and leadership – Okay – let's do this.

Day 3

I can't believe they're letting me touch them so much. It's crazy, it seems that I can enter their personal space whenever and however I want to. These creatures must not have the same boundaries in their culture. Also, if I ask them to pet me they do it without delay. When we go outside to explore I am able to lead the whole experience. If I persistently pull while simultaneously ignoring them I can then lay claim to the neighborhood trees and scent mark the entire area.

Day 4

They are encouraging higher energy levels in me – bizarre. Mom always stopped excess energy and wasted energy right away – these guys seem to promote it. When they enter the domain they make excitable sounds and let me jump all over them and socially groom and control them. I may even start escalating it a bit further as I am seeing a clear pattern.

Day 5

So far, I've gotten a load of treats and a ton of food – not bad at all. These tall creatures sometimes make me put my rear end on the ground and then give me the food – I find this odd and unnecessary. If they don't offer me some form of food I figure I'll just keep ignoring them like I usually do.

It's pretty quiet in the habitat and so far nobody comes to the door. I've started to lay claim to that area and the back yard. No one is going to be coming in except my two immediate companions from now on. I might be too nervous if someone new did try to enter.

I'll still play it cool for another week or two because this place is so new to me but it's becoming painfully obvious that I will be able to run the show here. I have memorized the environment, I have learned their habits and movements, and am sure I can lay claim to it all. If I increase my touches and keep claiming more possessions in this habitat soon I will be the real shot-caller. Yes, sir, not bad at all.

- Rover the rescue dog

Were you able to take a glimpse into a very different culture as you were reading Rover's journal above? We need to cultivate a much greater awareness when it comes to our partnership with the dogs if we hope to prevent or reverse behavior issues.

Dogs live with us, and not just in the barn like several other domesticated creatures, but in our very homes. They have lived with us for several millennia. Many dogs even sleep in our bedrooms or with our children. So why is there such misinterpretation and misunderstanding of their language?

The companion dog of today is in desperate need of real understanding and then a bit of proper leadership. Both are sorely lacking and it shows. Just Google some dog bite statistics if you don't believe me. Research some of that and you'll be adequately shocked and hopefully turned on to this overwhelming yet generally accepted or ignored problem.

I know we can do better than what the status quo is offering in the way of human behaviors and beliefs concerning our dogs. I know we can do better when it comes to the industry of dog training and behavioral modification. If we can only open our eyes to really see the situation for what it truly is, great results are waiting just around the corner.

Loving affection can be fantastic. I'm all for real love. But if we want a deeper connection, a deeper bond, a healthy and happy relationship for both parties, we need understanding and clear communication in order to have real love in the relationship with our dog.

"True love is born from understanding." Buddha

Is it possible to love someone or something without having a clear understanding? I think so. Is the love "truer" or richer or deeper with a clear understanding? Certainly!

We need to understand our dogs better. We need to understand where we are at this point in time and where the vast majority of our dogs fit in at this point in time. **It matters not where they used to be** (employed as our workers for thousands of years). If we love our dogs then why is there so little knowledge about their language and the way they would do things calmly and naturally?

When we examine the majority of dog training methods, why so little emphasis on calmness and proper peaceful movements in the environment and yet so much emphasis on excitable raw obedience? We need clearer understanding in order to truly love and intelligently direct our affections in a healthy and beneficial way.

We need to consider the other party instead of just ourselves, and how badly we feel about the poor rescue dog we just adopted. Feeling bad doesn't help our dogs.

The "poor and abused" rescue dog has many struggles to overcome. <u>Often our misdirected affection mixed with a terrible imagining of past tortures the dog may or may not have experienced only serve to keep the dog from moving forward with their new life</u>! Please re-read that last sentence. Think about it.

Of course this is not true of all cases, but were you aware that many rescue dogs that display skittish behavior around men most probably were not abused by men! Yes. You read that correctly. What was most probable was that the dog <u>greatly lacked normal socialization throughout its life</u>. Perhaps it was left at home during critical socialization periods all while growing at an incredible rate. The dog missed out on significant social dynamics and social normalcy through interacting with other people. The previous owner probably did not get the dog touched and handled by enough people. So fear crept in and built a stronghold.

When a dog is only <u>skittish around men,</u> instead of imagining horrendous past tortures we must consider things from a dog's point of view. Having helped thousands of fearful dogs I firmly believe many of these skittish cases occur because men are often larger and physically stronger than women. In many cases men have a deeper voice, and will walk right up to a dog directly in an attempted greeting. Keep in mind dogs, like all creatures in nature except for today's human being, don't give a fig about political correctness, what the TV or news reports, or the current trend in what or how people are being conditioned to think. Animals don't care at all about those things.

Our dogs calculate movement. They calculate size and strength.

They listen for tone. They notice eye contact. And if fear, phobias, or anxiety are present in a dog, the dog will quickly attempt to pick a person who will comfort that fear and nurture it – even if it's unhealthy and hurts them psychologically in the long run! The fearful dog is like an addict – always looking for a fix.

Nobody nurtures like our moms. Testament to the nurturing mother can be witnessed daily throughout nature in a multitude of species. While both parents can and should nurture their young, the mother is the absolute best in that category. On the opposite end, the father, in the overwhelming majority of mammalian cases, typically takes the cake when it comes to strength and fighting. In this way both parents lend their unique skills to and for the success of raising their young and seeing their genes survive another generation.

So when a nervous dog or pup is acting skittish around a man, unless that person approaching is legitimately a danger and threat, if one was to nurture or comfort the fearful animal at that moment that would only serve to make the fear grow! That would enable and encourage the distrust of men! Fear needs to be ignored or actively addressed with disagreement in most cases! But is this done? It is hardly ever done.

Please STOP LOVING your dog's FEAR

I've seen books in the dog industry that typecast a pup's personality as a "Nervous Nellie" or something to that effect. How damaging is this labeling psychologically speaking? How wrong? How terrible to label a dog's or anyone's personality as "fearful or nervous or skittish?" Doing that is a big problem. Fear is a thing that must be addressed and addressed for the better. Horrifically this will not occur if we simply say it's a part of their personality. No loving owner wants to erase or alter his or her dog's personality! So whoever wrote that book has been causing terrible damage to thousands and thousands of dogs for years now.

Congrats, you moron. If you are reading this please remember that there is help for your fearful dog or pup. It is NOT their personality. In truth, fear blocks a portion of their personality. Fear and skittish behaviors must be addressed properly if we desire future relaxation for yourself and relaxation and freedom for your dog.

Garrett's tip:

Fear can be greatly diminished in short order (in several cases) with the proper calming technique and a deeper understanding of how dogs actually move, think, communicate, and how dogs would naturally develop successful relationships among themselves. It has little to do with the external motivation found in mainstream training methods.

Fixing fear and reversing behavior issues in a dog **has little to do with analyzing past behavior**. Please re-read that last sentence. Past analysis may help correct fears in a human being, I don't know, but it most certainly hinders a dog's progress. Remember animals live in the moment with their amazing senses much more than we do with our big, distracted human brains and large frontal lobes. The fearful dog utilizes habits of fight or flight because somewhere in their past they found it worked for them. We, as dog owners, need to show them that fight or flight is now unnecessary and wholly unwanted except in an emergency. They need to move on with a clear understanding that they are now safe and a part of our family. **They cannot move on if we keep them as a victim in their past** by consistently treating them like they are still wounded! Please reread that one too. Think it over. What a huge disservice we do to our dogs if we constantly bring up their past. If things are legitimately "okay" in your dog's life now (meaning you've provided food, shelter, water, exercise, play and all the other things that make for a good life for your dog) then **there is zero need to keep telling the dog "it's okay!"**

Do you see why affection and praise and comfort or soft talk directed toward a dog or pup at the wrong time (wrong time would be whenever they're in a fearful state of mind) can be detrimental to their normal social interaction and their personal confidence? Misdirected human affection can make for a very strange and unhealthy relationship.

"Lord, grant that I might not so much seek to be loved as to love." - Francis of Assisi

Affection and love are amazing feelings and so necessary for a healthy relationship with a dog or with a person. So is understanding. So is proper communication. So are respect and trust and time spent together. We cannot exclude the other success ingredients of fun, enjoyment, curiosity, and play. They need to be included, too, for a lasting healthy relationship. To exclude them would be immature. Affection and love are the starting point and the main ingredient, but we need all the other components, too. When all the factors and ingredients are included that is a sure evidence of the maturity in the relationship. Be all-inclusive with your dog!

I hope you never coddle a dog like you would a human child when the dog is in a fearful state of mind because you may make the fear grow! Never keep your dog as a victim. Move forward boldly into the future.

CHAPTER 7 – MYTH 7

-Just give your dog a job to do

-Dogs need to work in order to be well behaved and fulfilled

"The end of labor is to gain leisure." - Aristotle

This myth is terrible. This generally accepted yet seldom questioned myth is truly horrendous! Everyone I've ever met, read about, researched, or talked to my entire life believes this myth! Everyone worships this false idol. Personally, even I used to believe in this myth! It's high time we questioned it. We must no longer pull our punches.

When there is a behavioral problem that just means your German Shepherd needs a job to do, correct? WRONG! Friends, this is ancient thinking. The main reason this myth is so prevalent is because dogs <u>were</u> employed since ancient times. The emphasis should be on the word "were."

Let me ask you, Dear Reader, <u>is your modern housedog employed currently</u>? Are the majority of pets across the world active in the military or police? Are the bulk of modern dogs actively guarding and shepherding large flocks of sheep? Are you a shepherd? Ol' Chap, are you the lord or duke of a manor that keeps large packs of well-bred dogs for the hunt? Are you the fine lady of a castle I'm not privy to that hunts her faithful hounds from the royal kennels while riding her favorite mount from the stables during an afternoon of jolly sport? Most probably...you are NOT!

Even if your dog does hunt with you, <u>nowadays dog owners want</u> **<u>more</u>** <u>from their dogs than just work</u>. They desire a **companion** that can, of course, obey, but even more importantly, that acts socially adept at home or in public. What we really want, which I find a bit humorous yet totally understandable, is for our dogs to act more like us! We want our dogs to act more like people. The good news is that we can actually have that, but we cannot get there if we keep thinking and viewing today's dogs like we did dogs from thousands upon thousands of years ago.

OUR COMPANION <u>DOGS ARE</u> <u>SEMI-RETIRED!</u>

Here's some wild counsel for you that goes 100% against the status quo...**<u>Stop</u> giving your dog or pup a "job to do."** <u>Stop</u> fixating so much on raw obedience training and you'll begin to discover and experience things differently in your relationship. New and better behaviors will occur in your home. You'll also <u>begin to bond closer to your dog than the lesser relationship of employer and employee.</u>

Did you know your dog or puppy is smart enough to perform obedience at the highest levels if given the training and yet somehow remain or become anxious, or aggressive, hyper, destructive, or unsocial? IT IS BECAUSE OBEDIENCE AND "JOBS" DO <u>NOT</u> ACTUALLY REVERSE OR ELIMINATE MANY BEHAVIORAL ISSUES!

Jobs and obedience training <u>add more tricks</u> and tasks; <u>they do not subtract behavioral problems efficiently.</u>

Example: There is a dog with some fear. The fears grow unchecked as the dog grows up in a loving human home because the owners were busy during the first year of ownership teaching the dog all sorts of tricks and obedience. The dog can now perform many wonderful commands. The dog can even perform a "sit" and a "watch me" command when the owner asks and yet be aggressive underneath the surface level of obedience. This means if you were to leave the scene and the dog was unattended, that dog would go over and attack another nearby dog even though the behaviorist has taught the dog owner and the dog the "watch me," and "sit," and other commands. Please think about that for a moment.

Another small example is the large numbers of dogs that are easily conditioned to enter their crate by way of a food treat and yet still remain riddled with separation anxiety. These are problems I see in homes every day and providing a job or task for the dog is not working to solve their problems.

I understand it sounds wild, but **more jobs and more obedience training is NOT what our dogs truly need to achieve better behaviors**! I'm attempting here to honestly illuminate a genuine problem for millions of households across the world. I am well aware that what I am detailing here goes against everything we've been taught thus far! I understand you may need to reread this chapter at some point and really digest it. This shocking info applies to our modern, companion dogs, despite what other professionals may say.

Obedience and giving your dog a job only focuses on the external motivation of the animal but in no way concerns itself with the more influential and powerful internal motivation! For more life-altering info on external motivation versus internal motivation, please read my book, _Talking Not Training: Forget Reinforcing your dog – Focus on Relationship_, and Daniel Pink's excellent book _Drive_.

The housedog of today needs calmness NOT more work!

Examining the myth:

Imagine if I gave you, personally, a few more jobs to do today. Would you need more energy to accomplish the tasks or less? You'd need more. Now let's ask someone struggling with their dog and struggling with problematic behaviors, do you wish your dog had more energy? Do you desire to add more energy to the dog displaying the problem? The answer from any dog owner with half a brain should be a resounding, "NO!"

Our puppies and dogs need more calmness to get along socially with other dogs and to function socially with people in the environments they find themselves in today. They don't need more energy. They certainly don't need to pass or transfer the energy from one behavior to another by performing tricks and commands. That is just juggling the energy but not actually calming the dog down and solving the issue!

This simple logic, tragically, is lost on many a professional trainer and behaviorist. It is lost on many a well meaning veterinarian and groomer. It is lost on the majority of dog daycare owners. Unfortunately, they are stuck in a very old, inefficient box. Sometimes their box is called "training." Other times the box is labeled as "behavior modification," or "modern training." In reality, it is the same-old-same-old. My suggestion to you is to leave them there. Leave them in their outdated boxes with these antiquated dog myths.

Let's move on into the future with the understanding that the mass majority of our dogs across the nation are in truth "semi-retired" housedogs. The main bulk of dogs in our homes are simply our companions. I don't think most folks would argue with that fact. For the most part our dogs, even the working breeds, are companion dogs in need of calmness and a healthy relationship in order to live wholesome, fulfilling lives and in order to function smoothly in society.

Behaviorally speaking, **calm sociability is always the answer** no matter what the question. This is because dogs are such a wonderfully social species. Any professional whose recommendation to you is something to the tune of "maybe your dog shouldn't ever be around other dogs" or "no one needs to touch your dog because it is **your** dog" is giving you and your family dangerous and absolutely awful advice! They are setting you up for greater liability. Anyone giving that sort of advice is suggesting you shrink your already problematic dog's social circle. Do you know what happens to a social creature if they are placed in solitary confinement? They go insane! Beware shrinking your dog's social circle. Don't do that to your dog. Beware bad advice! Some professionals would counsel you to keep your dog like a loaded weapon but there's a vast difference between our dogs and an inanimate tool like a firearm. When's the last time you heard of a gun lunging out the doorway and running up to shoot the neighbor? Dogs are living, breathing, and social creatures. Let's not fall prey to this classic dog myth by masking underlying behavioral issues through extra obedience and work! The truth will out.

Garrett's tip:

Here's a novel idea. Let's look to the dogs and their specific language and parenting skills to help influence our own dogs. Too often we look to the scientist and their selective studies in the sterile laboratory. Too often we look to the veterinarian for behavioral advice even though it's **not** their specialty. (Nothing wrong with asking, of course, but wouldn't the wisest thing to do when contemplating answers to dog language and behavior, be to look to the dogs themselves?) Too often we look to behavior modification techniques (positive or negative) that often amount to nothing more than bribery with food to harsh, overboard handling. Let's move on together. Let's all look at our dogs body and posturing. If we can grasp canine communication and actual dog language that would significantly diminish the need for extraneous work!

The mother and father dog teach their growing pups control of their own energy, which leads the pups down the path of **self-control**. They need their pups to keep their energies at social levels so fights don't break out and so they can function together efficiently as a family. They need clear communication. Because dogs have large families and due to large litters of puppies, the dog parents cannot micromanage their puppies or the pup's "work" so they offer freedom. Whenever the energy levels of an individual puppy are raised to too high a level, the parents intercede and address it by calmly (yet psychologically firmly) controlling the movement and space of the pup for a moment. To do this requires proper movement, posturing, and great timing. Sometimes it requires touching. Other times it does not. Then, as the energy drops back to socially acceptable levels, they (the parents) back off and start using their excellent tool of ignoring/trusting again. They give the pup freedom. It is quite amazing the amount of freedom dog parents give their young because it's much more than we, as human moms and dads, ever would. The mother and father dog tap into proven leadership skills. The parenting skills of any social dog are remarkable. In my opinion, as a father of three young children, we, as human parents, could and should collect as much information from nature and our dogs as possible. It is a great boost for our own parenting skills and for our relationships with our kids.

CHAPTER 8 – MYTH 8

-You just need to show the dog you're the Alpha

-My dog tells other dogs he's the Alpha by not putting up with anything

"Leadership is action, not position." – Donald H. McGannon

After spending countless hours working with and around our dogs, a new world of curiosity and discovery opened up for me. Over the years, I steadily and quite naturally began seeing trends and identifying problems within the dog training industry. As I kept learning the intricacies of the dog language and their social dynamics and how dog manipulations were applied on us, as people, I was amazed. I kept asking more questions and kept finding more effective answers in the dog's responses. Quite naturally I began mentally switching from what the known science was, what the animal behaviorists and the dog trainers teach and do, to questioning and examining them.

As an ENTJ (my results from the Myers-Briggs personality test) personality type, efficiency and proper leadership is totally my bag. I truly desire and have a psychological need in my personality to seek out and put into practice the most excellent ways forward in order to yield the greatest results. I have a need to lead. So I questioned, pondered, and saw with my own two eyes what, how, and why the dogs do what they do in their parenting and leadership techniques versus what mainstream dog trainers and behaviorists teach people to do. Lamentably, the two frequently didn't line up! The way of the mainstream dog trainers and behaviorists certainly didn't connect with the way of the mother and father dog (or with the way of any older, balanced, social dog).

Training, as we've gone over throughout this book, goes against Mother Nature as it pertains to calmness versus excitement and how leaders directly influence energy levels. (By the way, if you don't think leaders direct and influence energy levels and responses, please observe any good leader. Abraham Lincoln, Teddy Roosevelt, Winston Churchill, Martin Luther King Jr., Mother Teresa, Steve Jobs, or even Tony Robbins spring to mind.)

In my day-to-day business we basically help influence our client's thinking and their human behavior with reference to their dogs, which then leads to a reversal of their dog's behavioral issues. **I've discovered that training and behavior modification is NOT the most efficient way to do that in the most efficient time period in nearly all cases!** You may think this is a bit crazy, but I know the dogs (and our results) speak clearly for themselves and would verify these findings. Our clients certainly verify this, particularly those clients who have used many other forms of mainstream training techniques before finally finding our calming communicative methods.

The status quo is often wrong or at least so drugged up, dumbed down, beaten down, or distracted with a digital device that the next big discovery, or invention, or business could be right under our noses and we'd still want to keep doing things "the way they've always been done." The majority will always be for, "business as usual." After learning from the dogs and thinking about where we are in world history today with our dogs, I believe the alleged "modern" dog training industry of today is behind.

Alphas are dominating the heck out of everyone and everything, right?

The dominance (alpha wolf) theory concerning wolf behavior was introduced by Rudolph Schenkel in the 1940s and was furthered by David Mech in the 1970s. As many of you know, this theory of a rough alpha canine fighting his or her way to the top of the pecking order was disproved. This theory has been disproved both in wild wolves and in domestic dogs, yet many trainers are still spouting off about being an Alpha to your dog.

Why would some trainers do this? I suppose it is because they are implying to potential future clients that some dogs call for a sterner form of leadership in order to achieve decent results behaviorally throughout their life. I would agree with them on that. On the other hand, if it is because they are unthinking, harsh handling, hang, or roll the dog onto its back-type-trainers then I would, of course, disagree with them. As discussed, one can ruin a perfectly good dog through harsh handling.

Some pups are born to lead and it is evident from a young age when observed among their littermates. They are usually calmer. These pups may require a firmer constitution from the owner when introducing the house rules.

The main problem occurs with people's <u>definition of an alpha</u>. Thanks in large part to many overcompensating young men striving to make it in this highly competitive world, and thanks in part to the occasional muscle-bound meathead posing as an "alpha male" while simultaneously displaying poor decorum, weak conversation skills, and intellectual ineptitude, this image, unfortunately, has greatly influenced our definition and concept of the word. This mythological image has been furthered in popular media. The word "alpha" itself has been corrupted in our mind. As humans we cannot cut our ties and definitions to the human language, culture, and society, so we invariably end up defining an "alpha" as a power-hungry jerk that pushes everyone else around, takes no prisoners, and never apologizes. Nothing could be further from the truth pertaining to the mysterious and misunderstood alpha dogs that I believe exist in the dog world and are phenomenal communicators and peacekeepers. .

Positive-only trainers and fanatics despise these sorts of "alpha" trainers or even folks who use the phraseology "alpha" and continuously bash them. The internet is heavy with evidence of their wasted energy and petty attacks. Sometimes professional trainers who employ other methods besides those labeled as "positive only" fire shots back at the "positive only" folks. It goes on and on back and forth and vice-versa. Simple Google searches will reveal much evidence on this end.

Personally, I'm not in either extremely common camp that the majority of professional trainers and behaviorist find themselves in. **One should never need to give outrageous amounts of food treats to enhance performance from an animal, just as one should never need the use of shamefully harsh handling in order to control an animal.** Please, please remember, Dear Reader: These mainstream techniques of <u>positive or punitive</u> motivation are **purely <u>external</u>** and in no way as powerful or beneficial as **internal motivation!** The "positive only" methods and or the punitive, harsh handling techniques are both ineffective and insignificant <u>when compared to methods based in dog communication!</u>

Examining the myth:

I say alpha dogs exist! And while our human semantics and terminology isn't that critical as far as living a good life or having a great relationship with a dog, I also KNOW for a FACT that the masses maintain outrageous beliefs in how they define an "alpha" dog. Anybody who desires to find an alpha-type dog can usually observe them in action at your local dog park or busy dog daycare. And, shock of all shocks…<u>alphas are usually NOT the dogs that one would find snapping at other dogs, consistently growling at other dogs, assertively barking at other dogs, or knocking them down. They are NOT characteristically pushy or abrasive. They are NOT aggressive.</u>

If I were to give my <u>simplest definition of an alpha dog it would be synonymous with the word **parent**</u>. Alpha dogs are super effective communicators and behave like caring parents or grandparents. They are **calm, confident, and competent**. They spread these amazing characteristics to the dogs and environment around them. They have a calming influence.

True alpha dogs do **not** need to relentlessly control the circumstances around them because they are not motivated by a fearful state of mind. They will **not** be found policing the dog park by stopping play when other dogs or pups run near them. That is just another common dog myth. <u>True alpha dogs do not need to prove anything to anyone</u>. Isn't that interesting?

> **"It's none of my business what people say of me and think of me. I am what I am and I do what I do. I expect nothing and accept everything. And it makes life so much easier." - Anthony Hopkins**

Alpha dogs are **not** always the biggest or strongest in the park. However, they are the strongest mentally and display a superior grasp of peaceable communication. If they need to intercept a rising, unbeneficial energy from an errant dog nearby, alpha dogs will take the smoothest way possible and apply the least energy possible to resolve the situation.

Clear communication is a must for the alpha dog. They never growl when a simple look will do. They never stare if they can ignore. They have a highly developed and enhanced form of body language when compared to other dogs and it is a joy to observe an alpha's communication skills in action. Self-assurance is their stock in trade. True alphas know what's good for their family.

Alpha dogs can be observed helping calm drama and instill greater levels of peace. I've noted several alpha-type dogs that attempt to help out when a human interacts with a wayward dog. They will come right over and try and split up the tension by placing their body a certain direction. Their movements are superb for encouraging sociability and greater interaction. Selflessness and sharing is the name of the game for a genuine alpha.

"But he that is greatest among you shall be your servant." - Jesus

Garrett's tip:

Attempt to find alpha-type dogs on a busy day at the dog park. As you learn more of the dog language they will become easier to spot. (I suggest utilizing Turid Rugaas's book *Calming Signals: On Talking Terms with Dogs* to help you learn more of the dog language – while I don't agree with everything in the book, it is overall right on).

For your pup or dog:

Socialize, socialize, and socialize. That doesn't mean just take a group obedience class or two. Socialization means constant exposure to new and novel stimuli and somewhat awkward situations. Socialization will aid in the development of your dog or puppy's language skills. Socialize for success. The more we socialize the more we get a "dog." The more we socialize the less wild and wolfish behaviors come out. If we want less aggression or fear or anxiety, if we want more good behavior and less bad behavior, then we must expose and desensitize our dogs to the world. They must become well traveled and worldly.

I don't know if it's possible to lead a dog into becoming an alpha, but I am exceedingly sure it is possible to lead a dog into excellent communicative and behavioral skills and a healthier life overall.

CHAPTER 9 - MYTH 9

-Tugging with a dog can make them mouthy or possessive.

-You must win if you play tug of war with your dog.

"Don't wear roller skates to a tug of war." – Larry Wall

One of the hands-on techniques I usually implement whenever a client has a dog that is possessive and aggressive is to engage in tug of war. Probably not for the reasons you might think.

We play tug of war because it's fun. We play tug of war because it's play. We play tug of war because I can show the client and the dog how to escalate and pump up the energy and then how to deescalate the energy smoothly. We play tug of war because it takes place in MY spatial bubble. We play tug to help the dog drain energy. We do NOT play tug of war to "win" and beat the dog. We do NOT play tug to let the dog win and beat us. It is a stinking game.

> **"I will not play tug o' war. I'd rather play hug o' war. Where everyone hugs instead of tugs, Where everyone giggles and rolls on the rug, Where everyone kisses and everyone grins, and everyone cuddles, and everyone wins." - Shel Silverstein**

I love Shel Silverstein. We have most of his books in our house. As a boy I even had his tape and loved listening to him sing, play his guitar, and perform his poetry. But Shel is not a dog. Shel is not a dog behaviorist or a dog trainer either.

Healthy and psychologically balanced dogs greatly enjoy tug of war. It can be a superb way to interact, simultaneously raising levels of relaxation, burning excess energy, working a bit of training, and playfully bonding through touch, movement, and the space around our bodies.

Tug of war reveals much about your relationship

"You can discover more about a person in an hour of play than in a year of conversation." -Plato

Dogs reveal their relationship towards a person in the way they move with them and around them. They reveal how the relationship is doing through the space in the environment and how they give and receive touch. They reveal how they feel and think through their many actions and movements. They reveal much during play. If your puppy or dog is trying to be manipulative, you'll see it clearly during tug of war. They reveal much, if one knows what to look for. It is fairly easy to read a dog during the game tug of war.

Examining the myth:

The myth that playing tug of war makes a dog more possessive, or dominant, or aggressive is pure unadulterated horse crap. Please don't buy this myth or sell it to anyone else ever again. The foolhardy thinking goes something like this, "If you teach and train your dog to pull against you, well, then you are training the animal to fight you for things. That leads to possessive behaviors." Don't buy that line of thinking because playing tug of war can be much more beneficial for your relationship and the dog's obedience skills than playing fetch. Yes, tug of war is better than fetch.

Tug of war is a game of strength, skill, maneuverability, space, and touch if played properly. Tug of war should be very fluid and moving. Tug of war is filled (or should be) with differing movements around the space near the person's body, not the same tired, predictable, (and easily manipulated) movements that occur during a game of fetch. When a dog fetches it is a good sign of a dog's willingness to work for and interact with the owner if the fetch is clean and properly brought all the way back to the thrower's hand. Tug of war, though, has energy escalation and de-escalation values and reveals dog language through space and movement. These are important foundational things in canine communication that far surpass the movements in an extremely predictable game of fetch. Tug of war can also help your dog learn how to release the rope/tug/stick/ball very nicely. Tug of war can help train a pup or dog to carry something. Tug of war even helps if one wants to build up to or improve the game of fetch, particularly for a dog or pup that won't fetch at all. Playing tug the right way can improve the "Come" command and the, "Sit," "Down, and "Heel." Tug of war can be amazing and is one of the best forms of "play training" that exists. The problem is, I haven't seen many people that play tug of war well.

Garrett's tip:

Dog owners will play tug of war and let the dog tug them into their dog's space. This is no good. We need to <u>play backwards</u> and draw the dog into OUR personal space. Over the years I've noticed that many dog owners will play tug of war and hardly ever use two hands. This is no good either. Use the second hand to sometimes increase the speed and power on the tug/rope. Use the second hand to pat the head of the dog and playfully smack the ribs of the dog all while pulling on the tug/rope.

Simple test: If you cannot reach your dog's ribs easily to playfully smack them, please recognize that you are being outmaneuvered and your dog is acting in a controlling manner. If you cannot touch your own dog during play with your second "free" hand (the hand not on the rope or tug) because your dog will playfully slip away from your touch, you can know for sure you are being outmaneuvered and your dog is playing rudely. If any puppy or dog is continuously manipulating the space and touch during the game of tug of war, behavioral issues will be evident in other areas of the dog's life. If your dog or puppy strives to keep their muzzle/head above the rope/tug and pointed down at the ground during play they are revealing a rude or controlling attitude. Instead of sharing in a game of tug with you, they are showing you they think they should be able to possess or claim the item and you should be the one to give it over and release it. Do NOT give it over at that moment. Instead, adjust the muzzle and the position in which your game of tug is being played. Do not let the dog climb on you, or climb on the item being tugged, or on your arms. This head down claiming of the tug movement is often accompanied with paws placed on the tug or on the person's arms. Don't let that happen. It's okay to reset.

Think spatially. Think about touch. Think like a dog. We don't want to teach our domestic dog to act like a wild animal and avoid our spatial bubble or our friendly touch! If your dog is not in your spatial bubble when he is playing you are doing it wrong. Our dogs need to be in our personal space bubble for both party's success in the game. To me, when the pup or dog is comfortable playing in the spatial bubble and being touched while the energy is escalated, that clearly signifies trust and understanding and it will prevent doggy manipulation from being perpetrated on the hapless yet well-meaning owner. So play tug of war! Your arms should seldom if ever be extended all the way out during tug; keep your elbows bent as this keeps the dog in closer. Do not let the dog constantly flop over on the ground and do not let the dog climb you in a manipulative attempt at gaining the high ground. You should play slightly bent over and not standing fully erect. You should play "hard to get" by moving backwards. Turn sideways (away from the dog) to lure them into your space. Focusing the tug and the area of play in front of your body is the key. Occasionally hop backwards (I mean you should be backing up from time to time so the dog can come forward to you) and keep drawing the dog's head into the centerline of your body.

CHAPTER 10 – MYTH 10

-Dogs just want to please us

"I have learned that pleasing everyone is impossible but pissing everyone off is easy and fun." - unknown

Have you ever heard of this common myth? Perhaps you yourself even spread this one in casual conversation? If we're being honest the majority of us probably have!

I am here to announce <u>many dogs do NOT want to please us</u>! Many dogs want to please themselves!

Now, Dear Reader, please understand there are, of course, exceptions. The stereotypical golden retriever comes readily to mind. But even that faithful Fido typically took some guidance, socialization, and training initially. Someone had to cultivate a bit of respect and trust and communication within the juvenile dog. If I were to put a loose percentage on the number of dogs that <u>want to please us</u> versus those that <u>prefer pleasing themselves,</u> I believe it would shock you. My estimate on those pups or dogs that have a natural propensity to want to please us in this day and age would be a mere 20% - 25%. The other 75% - 80% of dogs would rather just do whatever the heck catches their fancy. And, as social and intelligent creatures, why not? Why would they want to please modern mankind? Why would dogs want to please someone that doesn't seek to understand them or communicate clearly with them in their own dialogue?

"Dogs just want to please." Give me a break. That's almost as preposterous as saying children just want to please! If we searched for a bit we would indeed find some children that naturally desire to please their parents and that seldom give their school teachers or future employers any trouble whatsoever. And if we look again we would see many other kids who generally just want to please themselves.

Now imagine these children taken from their birth parents and put into an entirely different habitat to be raised by an entirely foreign species surrounded by a different language, different customs, different physical senses and movements, different everything – possibly like sending our kids to live on Mars with the Martians. This, I think, is a more accurate portrayal sensually and communicatively speaking of what our pups experience when they come to us. There are some big differences between Homo sapiens species and Canis lupus familiaris to begin with. Add to those preliminary differences this pervasive mythology that is rooted in our thinking and behavior towards the dog and one can continue down the path seeing disconnection after disconnection in interspecies communication.

Doesn't this "wanting to please" dog myth set the hopeful new puppy owner or dog adopter up for failure from the get go? Because we initially believe that "dogs just want to please us" we are even more alarmed and disarmed to find out that a good number of them do NOT want to please! This myth psychologically positions scores of good people up for crushing defeat. This is why I've included this myth in the book.

Instead of talking honestly about the amazing physical and mental persistence and the potential manipulative power and social intelligence of our dogs and puppies from the get-go, we all keep it real surface level and chat about how much dogs need jobs and want to please us. I hope one day we can see how absurd that belief is. I think the only people who would deny this "please us" myth would be those fortunate dog owners who have only ever had great dogs that have naturally had the desire to please. Yes, they do exist. Just as people all over the world win the lottery. I'm not denying it. I'm simply trying to look out for masses of individual dog owners or those that hope to one day get a dog. We need to be prepared for all contingencies. We need to be prepared for an animal that might not want to please us. It's become exceedingly and overwhelmingly clear that many of us are totally off our rockers when it comes to our dog logic and how we let our dogs treat us.

Examining the myth:

You just rescued a Pit bull mix from a kill shelter in Los Angeles. Congrats on saving a life. But you falsely believe this common dog myth that the animal would want to please you. When he performed a few simple tricks in return for food payment at the shelter you were sold on this myth and on a couple others as well. Introducing your Pit mix into the home went relatively smoothly for the first few weeks but now the honeymoon is over. He's started to lunge after other dogs when on leash. He doesn't listen at home at all unless you've got a treat in your hand and he's really close to you. What happened? Wasn't he supposed to please you? Aren't you the "master"?

Let's make this really simple. In the dog training industry if you want your dog to please you then you better be prepared to pay. That's it. That's why this "please us" myth exists. That goes hand in hand with some other dog myths about food somehow being positive and how training with food is allegedly this amazing and modern (it's **not,** by the way) technique to train. Paying someone for anything as a rule can diminish the relationship and put a damper on the dog's internal drive and motivation. This is especially true in the long run. How can one build the internal relationship and communication skills when focused only on external motivation? If I were to pay my wife to love me, is that the sign of a healthy relationship? If I were to consistently pay my children to obey, does that mean we have a great relationship? Am I a great Dad? Do they respect and trust and love me? Do you see my point? Again, we must go back to asking how dogs do things, and what they do, and, of course, why they do them.

Now imagine paying your employees and they still don't want to please you! Does this happen in business? Undoubtedly it does. Is it good for the company? No. Is it good for the employer? No. Is it good for the employee? No. Not in the long run.

Having a healthy relationship includes the desire to please the other party. But which comes first, the chicken or the egg? Does the desire to please somehow come before relationship? Or does the relationship, which should be based in communication, mutual interests, body language, and play, develop into each party desiring to please the other? Relationship, by definition, is the state in which objects or people connect. It is the state of being connected. When we go into a relationship expecting to be pleased but seldom consider how to be a good pleaser to the other party, that is an association doomed to disconnection and failure.

Sometimes we must please those that are important to us in order to be pleased ourselves. There is always a balance if one looks for it. Please don't take this too far. Personally, I am the last person on earth that would be labeled a people-pleaser. If anything, I lean towards the other side of that coin, but for any relationship to exist in the long run between people or dogs it must be a two-way street. Practically speaking, this in no way means giving your rescue dog or puppy every little thing it desires all at once. On the contrary, it means striving to give the dog a healthy relationship, as dogs would build one, with boundaries and authentic attempts in speaking the same language.

My wife and I speak the same language. My kids and I speak the same language. Daily I attempt to learn and to speak the language of the dogs (with my dogs) and I expect them to learn something of human linguistics as well. This is the quest for real communication. This is the quest for genuine connection.

Garrett's tip:

If you are looking to bond and connect with your dog on a deeper level you have got to turn down excessive human talking and turn up your human vision. Use your eyes more than your mouth when interacting with your dog. Observe. Watch. Learn. This is crucial. It's okay to guess at their body language occasionally, just beware, letting your guesses and theories crystallize. Remember, the dog language is fluid and flexible and sometimes one sign or posture as seen through a human lens can mean one thing and another time it can mean something completely different. Learning some of the dog language will help you please your dog and your dog will then be much more likely to want to please you in return.

Even more important to your dog than bridling the human tongue and using your eyes would be learning to touch your dog properly. Skillful touching is the absolute best way to bond with and please your dog or pup. Touch is every pup's first sense of the world. Touch has the power to translate us into an entirely different world. Touch bridges the great gaps that divide our cultures and species. Touch is always where connection can be seen and celebrated or where disconnection becomes more and more obvious. Whenever or wherever selfishness has entered in the relationship it can be revealed through how our dogs give or receive touch!

I suggest practicing many forms of touch and non-touch with our dogs. Not letting a dog touch you and playing "hard to get" by ignoring them can aid greatly in raising respect. By not allowing your dog to touch you helps to drive the "attention hound" habit out of your dog and also helps with recall ("Come" or "Here" command) when you do finally give the dog attention and decide to call him.

When you pet your dog or puppy, be sure to massage, knead, rub, scrub, lightly smack, ruffle, lightly push, lightly pull, grab, turn, nudge, and whatever other words you can think of to describe differing touches on various spots of their body. The more varied the touches are, the better, as this greatly enhances the dog's understanding that his body is nothing to guard (unless being attacked). I often will use my hand as a sort of dog tongue or dog teeth and will pet or massage them that way. This sort of handling really helps to keep everyone in the society safe. The behaviorist will thank you, as will your vet, groomer, neighbor, long lost grandma, and the Girl Scout cookie sales gal at your front door. If we claim our dogs' bodies (and we should because of domestication, their neoteny, and our search for healthy relationships with calm, social dogs) then they cannot guard them or get possessive over other items.

CHAPTER 11 – MYTH 11

-Training my dog is the pinnacle of our relationship

-Training and/or Behavior modification leads to great relationship and great behavior

-If my puppy is trained he won't develop behavioral problems

"I am not spoiled. I just happen to be great at training people." - The dog

Let's be forthright. Steve Jobs said, "If you want to make everyone happy <u>don't be a leader – sell ice cream</u>." It is our challenge to be better leaders for ourselves, for others around us, and certainly for these dogs that we adore. <u>The myth in this chapter is the biggest myth of all</u>! Behaviorally speaking, this is Godzilla-sized!

As a dog trainer myself I may even be hurting future business if this book catches on like we are anticipating. There is a slight element of personal danger here. I may be cutting back on the overwhelming need for training and behavior modification in general in the future. Probably not, though, due to so much terrible dog training and dreadfully misguided information on dogs that exists en masse.

Dogs and pups need training, right? Many folks bring home a puppy and a month or three later they are in need of some training or behavioral guidance. So, in order to socialize and train, they sign right up for a group class. Other owners, desiring a more personal touch or better results, sign up for private sessions with a local trainer or behaviorist. And some dog owners just go it solo because they've raised other dogs before and already assume they know what to do. Maybe they do. Or maybe what they know worked with a past dog will not work with their new one. I don't know. What I do know is that <u>when we put things of secondary importance in a primary place in any area of life we often wind up backwards.</u>

The thinking behind this dog myth goes something to the tune of Obedience and training is the best way to bond with your dog and training prevents or eliminates behavioral issues. <u>The myth is that obedience and training is first and foremost in our relationships with our dogs or pups. This dog myth is that dog training IS our relationship. This myth propagates the belief that "because we train or use techniques to modify misbehaviors, the future dog will be well behaved."</u> **In reality, this is often not the case.**

We help countless clients who, before discovering our services, have utilized mainstream modification methods and dog obedience to no avail. Their dogs and pups learned tricks (They got the obedience basics down pat. They received certifications) but did **not** develop a healthy relationship with their owners in their daily interactions and communication. Sadly for many caring dog owners that's all their relationship is...surface level obedience. Please read on.

Now, do I want my dogs to obey? Yes, probably more than most people you'd ever meet in this world. I am, after all, a dog trainer. Is obedience and training important? Yes, again. It is important. Do my dogs have great training? They're older now, but they literally used to jump through hoops for me! My dogs used to throw trash away whenever I'd ask them to, guard the family on demand, and help unload the groceries from my truck by gently bringing bags of food into our kitchen and running back to my truck for more! That's just to name a few of the tricks and commands they know. Now, instead of all those tricks, my dogs truly help behaviorally rehabilitate other dogs suffering with dog-

dog aggression. They are canine ambassadors representing calm sociability.

Is obedience training and having our dogs work and perform for us the key to a healthy relationship? NO. No, Dear Reader, it is Not! Obedience is one way to bond, but it is naturally <u>not</u> the primary way!

In order to understand this concept we have to look at what obedience really is. Let's look at it simply and directly. The more simple and direct we are in our observations and in our actions, the closer we can understand and interpret our dogs, their specific language, and the beauty that lies in that honest approach to life. Please try it.

"Simplicity is nature's first step and the last of art."
- Philip James Bailey

What is dog obedience? What is dog training? Obedience is making a puppy sit its rear on the ground while we say the human word, "Sit." Obedience and or training is making a dog perform a "Stay" command on his/her bed in order to prevent annoying begging while we eat dinner on the couch. Obedience is a police-trained shepherd smelling and tracking a criminal on the run. Obedience is a chocolate Lab leaping into icy waters to retrieve a duck splashing dead into the pond.

Does the mother dog care about such things? Does the father dog care?

Do the birth parents (the natural born leaders) care at all if their pups perform a "Sit"?

Why on earth would they care if their puppies placed their bottoms on the ground when they heard the word "Sit"?

Do dogs communicate the same way with each other as we do as humans?

How do dogs bond with each other? Have you ever asked these questions?

These questions are critical. They are critical in our quest to dispel these many widespread dog myths. They are critical in giving us an honest look and a greater understanding of ourselves, our behavior, our nature, Mother Nature, and the beliefs and actions toward these dogs we all claim to love. So what does the mother dog care about? It certainly isn't most obedience and typical dog training or behavior modification, is it?

Let me be clear. Obedience, training, and behavior modification is important. The myth or problem occurs when we assume that it is everything or that it comes first. Countless people are totally unaware that **there are methods much greater than training and obedience for bonding with their dog**. There are specific techniques within the dogs' detailed language of touch, movement, energy, and spatial control that can prevent, reverse or alter bad behavior **much faster** than our generally accepted forms of obedience, training or behavior modification! Please think about that last sentence. Read it again. Let it sink in.

Examining the myth:

A frustrated dog owner calls the behaviorist to help reverse or cure her Rottweiler's dog aggression. The first meeting seems okay as the behaviorist feeds her dog treats and asks the owner questions. Unwittingly the behaviorist only looks to what he or she has been taught about obedience techniques and dog training. We can only draw from what we know, right? The problem is the results the behaviorist brings to the table are soon revealed to be shoddy to mediocre at best. Bribery by way of food soon becomes the order of the day as the behaviorist proceeds to load up the dog owner with food treats.

If we looked in on Step 2 of their behavior modification plan, we would find the dog owner making her dog perform a "Watch me" or "Look" command whenever her dog sees another dog and wants to attack it. This "Watch me" command requires the dog to look up at the owner's face and, if they do look up – and look away from the dog they want to attack - they'll receive payment/bribery. If the current food being used to pay/bribe the dog to look up isn't working, the behaviorist will then introduce a food that is even more delicious and tempting. Her dog is supposed to look up at her in the presence of another dog. **What happens in reality in the overwhelming majority of cases is usually a spectacle of ridiculousness all culminating in total frustration and humiliation on the part of the unwitting dog owner.** Meanwhile, the behaviorist, possibly unaware of better techniques and solutions or, possibly, unwilling to learn them, reassures their client that it's a long process and that the client needs to have more classes and sessions with her.

Let me ask you, in that very authentic, real life example above, would the mother or father dog do any of what the behaviorist or dog owner did? Would the mother dog seek to train or modify a behavior when she could simply "speak" instead? Would she pay or bribe her puppies or the dogs in her charge in order to elicit a certain behavior or to stop a behavior?

And here's another question for you. Are treats exciting to the dog? To most dogs: YES! Do we want to raise the aggressive dog's energy and pay/bribe it whenever it sees another dog? Where is natural movement in that behavior modification process? Where is dog language? Where is calmness?

Real relationship and real communication should always, always, always precede obedience training, or, in the very least, be taught at the same time. The big trouble is that up to now, as far as I know, the greater part of the human population substitutes training and obedience for language and communication.

Garrett's tip:

Dogs talk to each other **without** food. They build relationships at daycare and dog parks and family members' backyards **without** food. They don't harp on endlessly about positive reinforcement or negative reinforcement. They don't care about human's views of dog training and scientific behavior modification. Dogs can please each other without exchanging food. They care about communication and being calm enough to get along socially.

Concentrate on fluid movements and how dog language works and less on "training."

Focus on peaceful postures and the right angles and less on "work."

Consider how you move and how the dog's body moves and don't look so much to external items and tools in hopes of fixing behavioral issues.

Cultivate an exceptional heel with your dog. This means that dog should be able to walk beside you or slightly behind you without pulling on the leash and without releasing himself to go sniff something or attack something. Heeling not only drains energy in the mind of the dog but in the body as well. Heeling teaches your dog proper respect because the dog has an opportunity to follow your lead while on the walk. In a world without human interference, a wolf pup or feral dog pup would naturally follow his/her parents during the first year or two of life. Heeling lets your dog relax and mirror you. Heeling can aid your dog in getting closer to other dogs, people, or situations that it might not have been comfortable with initially. (We have a video that is available for purchase on our website that gives folks a great start on heeling with their dog or pup.)

Body blocking is another technique one must learn and employ properly if one desires to speak clearly with a dog. Love him or hate him, Cesar Milan taught this body-blocking move to the world. It is utilized to take space from a dog and to cause the dog's eyes to look up at the approaching/blocking person.

Eye contact is key for communication. Eye contact is also a key indicator of respect and trust between you and your dog. Paying for eye contact does NOT mean you have earned your dog's respect. Eye contact is also the key for de-escalating aggression or fear in a dog. Body blocking at the right moment can lead to eye contact without the need of food bribery. Body blocking means that you position yourself in front of the animal's face. Feel free to back them up if necessary as that causes a dog to raise their face. I often combine this body block posture and then switch the dog back into a heel position when working with an out-of-control dog.

Conditioning your dog or pup to receive oodles of touching from masses of dogs and people will make for a fantastic pet that is psychologically sound and socially well behaved. Never forget how vital touch is for achieving a balanced dog.

IN CLOSING

In the quest for an excellent relationship with our dogs and in order to prevent, reverse, and eliminate behavioral problems in any age dog, we must consider how dogs relate to one another. We must strive to put their point of view above our own for the purpose of understanding and the furtherance of interspecies communication. We must destroy the behavioral dog myths surrounding us wherever we find them, we must search for the truth in their language, and stop common canine manipulations. In this way we will help our dogs, ourselves, and others see the light.

> **"Courage is what it takes to stand up and speak.**
> **Courage is also what it takes to sit down and listen."**
> **- Sir Winston Churchill**

In this book I've done my best to point out the main problems in the dog training industry in hopes that great change could occur. Tragically for millions of dogs, these problems remain unchanged due to our misguided belief in the aforementioned dog myths! Let's change that, shall we? The answers to industry-wide problems are all around us if we open our eyes to our own dog's language. I've also practically detailed the common issues that a host of dog owners experience daily in their homes with their dogs and clear solutions to those. I've been honest and forthright. I hope you can appreciate that, even if some of the chapters in this book didn't feel good. Please keep in mind this book's purpose is for dispelling dog myths and diminishing problems by enhancing healthy relationship and communication the natural way. This book is for you, Courageous Reader, and it is written for your dog or pup.

Thank you for caring enough about dogs to take a different look at them and a bold look at our interactions with them. If you read this book you are now responsible for helping create a better future between dog and man! What an exciting time to be alive.

"The best way to predict your future is to create it."
–Abraham Lincoln

SPECIAL THANKS

My special thanks and appreciation to all those amazing folks who helped this book come together. Thanks to my wife and kids. Please forgive any closed doors or crankiness towards the end of writing this thing. I love you. Thanks to all the dogs and all our clients. *Dog Myths* would not be possible if not for you. Thanks to Robyn Carper for her patience and for her mad photo skills. Thanks to Charmi Keranen for her professional and punctual editing. Thanks to Gabe Aluisy and the team at Shake Creative for the great graphic work on the covers, spine, and everything else. Sincerely, I'm so thankful for you all.

For more info on Garrett Stevens, his custom relational rehab techniques, speaking engagements, upcoming books, or our remarkable dog training products please visit us at

www.gstevensdogtrainer.com

Garrett Stevens is an animal nerd and a nature lover. His interests include but are not limited to: pizza, knives, books, travel, snow, hiking, martial arts, and mango lassi (these are not necessarily enjoyed simultaneously). He is a husband to one of the most genial and gorgeous creatures to ever grace the planet. He is a father to three remarkable, life-filled, and loony children (with another wee one on the way) and two fun-loving and faithful boxers. Like a sasquatch, Stevens resides in the moist and mossy Pacific North West. Most often you can find him in or around the City of Destiny.

CPSIA information can be obtained
at www.ICGtesting.com
Printed in the USA
FSHW01n1334090218